José Echegaray, James Graham

The Son of Don Juan

An original drama in 3 acts inspired by the reading of Ibsen's work entitled

José Echegaray, James Graham

The Son of Don Juan

An original drama in 3 acts inspired by the reading of Ibsen's work entitled

ISBN/EAN: 9783337304102

Printed in Europe, USA, Canada, Australia, Japan

Cover: Foto ©Thomas Meinert / pixelio.de

More available books at **www.hansebooks.com**

The Son of Don Juan

*AN ORIGINAL DRAMA
IN 3 ACTS*

by

JOSÉ ECHEGARAY

Translated by JAMES GRAHAM

CAMEO SERIES

T. Fisher Unwin Paternoster Sq.
London E.C. MDCCCXCV.

José Echegaray: a Sketch.

BY JAMES GRAHAM.

THE author of the plays here done into English was born in Madrid on the Thursday in Holy Week of sixty-three years ago. In spite of a fair indication to go by, his friends are responsible for the curious assertion that he himself does not know, or has not taken the trouble to verify, the exact date of his birth. A reference to familiar sources of chronology enables us to make a respectful claim to better information on the point than the person most concerned. So the day of Señor Echegaray's birth may be fixed precisely as the 19th of April, 1832.

The first three years of the dramatist's life were passed in the capital of Spain. In 1835 he was removed from Madrid by his father, who had just obtained the appointment of Professor of Greek at the Institute of Murcia. It was in Murcia that José received the rudiments of his education; and while still a child he entered the institute. Here he studied Latin under Professor Soriano, Natural History under Angel Girao, and Greek under his own father. The boy was early seen to be gifted with brain-power of the first order. And being of a docile and amiable nature, of active and laborious habits, having the advantage of excellent tutors, and being under the supervision of a kind and cultured father, it is hardly to be wondered at that his progress in learning was great and rapid. From the first he displayed that passion for mathematics which has never grown cool in him throughout life. His interest in literature itself was far from absorbing. He showed, indeed, some liking for novels and romantic dramas. For tragic writers of the stamp of Corneille and Racine he could not conceal his disrelish, though the fairness of his mind would never permit him to ignore or deny the many beauties of the classic drama. When he was fifteen years old he became Bachelor of Philosophic Science, and proceeded to Madrid in the month of October, 1847, to prepare for entrance into the Escuela de Caminos. In this great school the mathematical professor was Angel Riguelme, under whose able tuition young Echegaray devoted himself with increased ardour to his favourite study. His affection for literature, it is true, had been gradually strengthening. In the midst of his graver studies he had also frequented the theatres. But he never failed to return with an almost frenzied delight to the branch of knowledge which afforded such food to his voracious intellect. To use his own language, he " studied the higher mathematics ferociously, ravenously." It has been maintained that in all the records of Spanish scientific history no one has ever been known to devote more eager and profound study to mathematics than José Echegaray. His whole spirit seemed to be inextricably identified with the subject, to be indissolubly enchained to it. Mathematics became for him the most absolute of necessities, the supreme of joys. The following is an experience related by a fellow student of Echegaray when both were at the Escuela de Caminos. "Every Saturday our professor of mathematics was fond of setting us problems of the most difficult kind, the solutions of which we were expected to hand in on the Monday. On a certain occasion the problem given out to us was of such an excruciatingly intricate nature that the huge majority of the class had to give up all hope of mastering it. I was among the unsuccessful ones. I had seen Saturday, Sunday, pass over without bringing me nearer to a glimpse of light. On the Monday morning I was all at once inspired with the idea of going to Echegaray to obtain some hint on a question which could not have failed to occupy his attention at least as much as mine. It was an hour before the time appointed for the opening of the Escuela and the delivering up of the answers. I set out for Echegaray's lodging. I found my friend in his room. The curtains were drawn and the shutters were fastened over the windows. On the chimney-piece was an expiring lamp. On the edge of the bed—the clothes of which were tossed about in much disorder —sat Echegaray in his nightshirt. His head was bent, and he was in an attitude of deep thought. The noise which I made on entrance was as unsuccessful as my friendly greeting in withdrawing him from his abstraction. He confined himself to raising his hand with a gentle but expressive motion, and to saying 'Hush!' Suddenly he bounded up, undressed as he was, and, to my stupefaction, exclaiming, 'Here it is!' hurried across to a small board close at hand. He commenced to draw lines upon lines and circles upon circles, and dash down figures here and there, till at length he said, 'The whole night have I been thinking of that problem, and— look there!' And he drew back to show me the signs all fairly traced, the operation completed, the problem solved. This rehearsed performance he repeated in school that morning. He alone did it, to the admiration and almost to the alarm of the professor himself, who, I think, had really given out the problem without much serious thought of any one even attempting a solution."

Echegaray had entered the Escuela de Caminos in 1848. He finished his course of study in 1853, carrying off with him the highest honours that the institution could bestow, and being placed far and away the first of all his contemporaries. Meanwhile the literary and dramatic instinct lay almost entirely asleep in him. It sprang up fitfully now and then in a curiosity to assist at the initiatory performances of pieces by first-rate, second-rate, and even third-rate authors. Echegaray was always held up as an exemplary pupil; he fulfilled his duties at school with almost exaggerated obedience and scrupulousness; and yet once—only once—he ran out of the Escuela de Caminos without permission that he might not be too late to buy tickets for the first night of Ayala's drama, "El Hombre de Estado." On leaving the Escuela, then, in 1853, Echegaray had already seen many dramas, and had read a vast number of French, English, Italian, and Portuguese novels, ancient and modern, of all kinds. But he had not himself essayed anything in literature. He had not written a verse. The making of verses appeared to him a thing quite foreign to his nature. In this the enemies of Echegaray are affable enough, for once, to agree with him; and they remain constant to their belief when he has long since had ample reason for changing his mind. The mathematical rigidity and angularity of much of his poetry, say these enemies, is not compensated for even by the daring originality of his conceptions, his nobility of sentiment, the richness of his imagery, the splendour of his language; they deny to him, for instance, the exquisite ease and melody of Espronceda, the bird-like spontaneity and perhaps fatal fluency of José Zorilla. In short, during these days of his dawning manhood, Echegaray had never dreamed of being a poet, still less a dramatic genius.

The requirements of his profession as tutor of mathematics, to which he now formally addressed himself, took him to various important cities— Granada, Almeria, Palencia—thus keeping him away for years from the capital, where he was destined to shine in whatever he undertook. At last the moment came for his return to Madrid. He was elected Professor of Mathematics at the Escuela de Caminos, at the very institution where he had achieved such triumphs as a boy and a young man, and where he had left behind him so many pleasing remembrances. And now his professional engagements, and the extraneous tasks which he voluntarily imposed on himself, scarcely left him time to breathe. During the thirteen years of his occupation of the mathematical chair an immense number of classes had the advantage of his teaching of the Infinitesimal Calculus, Theoretical and Applied Mechanics, Hydrostatics, Curve-tracing, Descriptive Geometry and its applications, Solid Geometry, and so on into the dimmest heights of the science. During this time he devoted himself to Political Economy, to Philosophy, to Geology, and to another study, entered upon with slight equipment by many men, very seriously and with all his faculties by this man—Politics. At the Bolsa and the Free Exchange Propaganda he delivered orations full of subtle thought and sound doctrine; in the Ateneo he spoke enthusiastically in favour of pure democracy; in presence of the Society of Political Economy he pronounced numerous discourses appropriate to their several occasions, and distinguished by an order of eloquence which was looked upon as remarkable, even in a capital where almost every one seems endowed with the gift of picturesque and ready speech. He published different articles in the *Economista*, *La Razon*, and other periodicals—it seeming impossible that he should give his attention to multitudinous labours of this kind, and at the same time devote eight or ten hours of his days and nights to private lessons in mathematics and to public lectures on other subjects, among which were Physics and Naval and Military Engineering. Such excessive work would have paralysed a nature less vigorous than Echegaray's, but in the continuance of a portion of it he was unexpectedly stopped. The private lessons which he had been giving would have raised an independence for him. They were prohibited. Echegaray was made a victim of the administrative despotism to which the authorities of the Escuela de Caminos were compelled to bow. He applied for a special license; it was refused. In his indignation he was about to leave the Escuela. But there he was assured that he would be acting ill-advisedly. If he indeed abandoned his career in defiance, he would forfeit all his rights as a tutor in the public schools of Spain. The earnest remonstrances of his friends, joined to the promptings of his own reason, induced him to relinquish the design. His most powerful motive against precipitancy was that he had not the heart to break with the work of his whole life. He was the soul of the Escuela. He had become indispensable, alike to his fellow professors and to his pupils. Mathematics consoled him for all his trials, and to them he continued to consecrate himself with a loving fervour which even he had never surpassed. The mathematical treatises which he then began to send forth in rapid succession from the press will not be readily allowed to die by the scientific world of Spain.

Being about this time commissioned by the Spanish Government to study the works of tunnel making at Mont Cenis, and having no opportunity of doing so at leisure on his arrival, a very brief inspection sufficed for him to understand, or rather to guess, the whole of the internal mechanical arrangements of the perforators. And, thanks to this, and without bringing away with him sketches or plans of any sort, he, on his return to Spain, drew up a memorial with the most detailed description—a description subsequently proved accurate in all essential particulars—of the mechanism and procedure employed in the enterprise.

All this while there had been nothing in Echegaray's tastes or performances that gave evidence of the poet, the dramatist, or even, in any distinct form, of the man of letters. His literary works, or rather such works of his as had even a suspicion of literary flavour about them, had been thus far confined to certain political orations, to articles on Political Economy, to publications on Mathematics, and to a humorous little sketch entitled, "The Comet, or a Carnival Joke," which appeared in a Madrid newspaper. Echegaray's partiality for the reading of novels and for the frequenting of theatres was the same. Still there was no awakening within him of any expressed ambition to write in emulation of those whose productions he admired as a spectator.

Towards the year 1864 it was that José's brother Miguel, then a mere lad, wrote a little piece in one act and in verse entitled, "Cara o Cruz," which was put on the stage, and was received in a friendly manner. And José, equally startled and amused at the spectacle of his boy brother writing smooth and harmonious verse, rapidly acquired the conviction that, after all, the writing of verses ought to have no stupendous difficulty about it. He did not long delay an experiment. He immediately set about putting together an appalling tragic argument, which he versified with tolerable ease. In this fashion was composed his first play. He kept it by him for a year. Having in the meanwhile dedicated himself with serious and characteristically energetic study to the whole question of dramatic writing, he drew the piece forth and read it a second time. He found it by no means equal to his first complacent judgment of its merits. He at once chose a safer hiding-place for it than previously, and it has never seen the light. Echegaray was becoming more and more immersed in these new subjects of interest, when an interruption came in the most notable public episode of his life. The revolution of 1868, and the flight of Isabella, launched him into the full tide of politics. His known ability naturally fitted him for the playing of a prominent part. He was very speedily selected for Cabinet rank in the newly-formed Government. He was created Minister for the Colonies. His new duties, entered upon and sustained with vigour and success, removed him for five years from the concerns of literature and the drama. Towards 1873, on the dissolution of the Permanent Commission of the Cortes, Echegaray's name was proscribed. He was in imminent danger of death. He escaped to France.

Eventually the ban was taken from his name, and his life was preserved, through the commanding influence of Emilio Castelar. This has been ever since gratefully acknowledged in a manner which does credit alike to the great orator and the great dramatist.

In the meantime, during his comparatively brief exile, Echegaray had written in Paris his drama, "El Libro Talonario." It is the first of his pieces which was put on the stage, and the date of its production is February 18, 1874—not long after the author's return to Spain. Nothing commonplace could come from Echegaray, yet neither in style nor in argument does the work give any revelation of the future greatness of the writer. Very little better was the reception accorded by the critics of Madrid to the second performance of the new poet, " La Esposa del Vengador," also produced in 1874. There was not one, however, who failed to admit the numerous beauties of either play. The third effort, " La Ultima Noche," again, was declared to be a chaotic conjunction of graces and monstrosities : as a work of genius unimpeachable ; as a display of true dramatic quality, absurd.

On the other hand, the public of Madrid, roused to the highest pitch of interest in the new career marked out for himself by the celebrated mathematician, the ex-Cabinet Minister, the returned exile, had been receiving one after the other of his dramas with delight. This was not enough for a man of such iron will as Echegaray. He was deliberately bent on subduing his critics. His three first dramas had been experiments. He had been merely trying his hand.

On the 12th of October, 1875, was produced " En el puño de la Espada." The play was welcomed with unanimous and boundless enthusiasm. The irregular and fiery genius, whose only enemy seemed to be his individual rashness, had stepped safely aside from down-rushing avalanches and gaping precipices, had scaled the heights reached by those few alone whose names will live, and was looking down in security and serenity alike on admiring critics and acclaiming public. From that night the severest judges of the Spanish capital recognised that there had come among them a dramatist of the first rank. Since that night Echegaray's career has been one long triumphal march, his path strewn with flowers, his eyes rejoiced with the smiles of countless friends, his ears greeted with cries and songs of praise—and envy.

One of the most noted peculiarities in the onward course of Echegaray is the mixture of patient scorn and fierce energy with which he declines to look upon difficulties as insurmountable. Not merely in the solution of a hard problem in mathematics, or in clearing from his path the impediments which now make him rule the theatre of Spain as a monarch, does Echegaray show the force of his will. The rough term in which Ancient Pistol sums up the attributes of the Spaniard of Shakespeare's time could not be more ludicrously applied than to such a man as José Echegaray.

In our country it is natural to conceive that we can pay no higher compliment to a man than by proclaiming him to be even as one of ourselves. Mr. Swinburne recognises — and with infallible justice—"a decisive note of the English spirit in Molière," as well as in Rabelais. In one way, at least, in the moral if not in the intellectual sense, in his resolution to ignore defeat, however incongruous be the task he may undertake, there appears to the observer of Echegaray's career something strangely

English. Two anecdotes may be given, alike as proofs of his almost boundless versatility, and of his constancy in breaking through seemingly impenetrable obstacles. On one occasion, he being in a drawing-room with several of his friends, among whom was a philosophical critic of some renown, the conversation fell upon German philosophy. Echegaray, who knew little of the matter discussed, and less of the German tongue, deemed it presumptuous to hazard an opinion for or against the thesis advanced, and maintained an absolute silence. Gradually, however, the debate resolved itself into a dispute as to the possibility of making an exhaustive study of a certain school of philosophy within a relatively short period. There can hardly be a more modest or amiable man than Echegaray, and yet the mere breathing of the word "impossibility" has been known at times to rouse him into an attitude of imperial defiance almost worthy of Cæsar or Napoleon. He left the house with the secret intention of proving that nothing is difficult to a man with clear brain and indomitable purpose. From that hour he devoted himself with patient zeal to no less a task than that of studying the special school of philosophy just argued about in the very fountains from which it emanated, in the original text of the German authors themselves. With such effect did he apply himself that, two months later, being in almost the same company, and the conversation—as the narrators will have it, with the usual emphatic pointing to coincidence—veering round to the same theme, the new student of philosophy displayed a depth of discernment, an acuteness of independent thought, a readiness of argumentative resource, a fertility of citation from the German language itself, which confounded the listeners; and apart from the congratulations on his new linguistic acquirement, there was an unanimous admission that Echegaray had expressed himself on the subject as a master in the midst of novices.

Another time he was in the company of friends who were engaged in a most exhaustive dissertation on the art of fencing. Innumerable were the experiences detailed in illustration of practice with the sabre, the sword, and the foil. Those who were least excited by the discussion turned now and then to Echegaray with a courteous explanation and a general air of respectful apology for treating of matters in which he could take no conceivable interest. Echegaray, in truth, had never held an offensive weapon in his hand. Next day, however, he appeared at the rooms of one of the best-known fencing masters of Madrid, enrolled his name as a pupil, and took his first lesson instantly. There are living eye-witnesses who tell how, three months afterwards, the grave mathematician, the coming lord of the Spanish drama, in a desperate encounter with foils, repeatedly hit, and at length actually disarmed his fencing master himself, amid the intense amazement and uproarious enthusiasm of bystanders, who counted among them some of the most expert fencers in the Spanish capital.

Echegaray's very career as a dramatist might in a measure be described as a gigantic experiment in the art of vanquishing difficulties, an elaborate and prolonged *tour-de-force*. He was a spectator of his brother Miguel's boyish and successful entrance into the domain of dramatic poetry. He saw nothing to prevent himself from following in the same path. His own prescription for writing verse is concise, and contains a justification of his new departure. He sums up the full requirements of a poet in " A little grammar, a little imagination, and a tolerable ear for music." This is a matter-of-fact style of putting things which may seem rather like a ruthless tearing aside of the veil from a sanctuary that should never be revealed to profane eyes. The great unpublished poets whose own works are the result of the purest inspiration will resent it accordingly. Yet there is reason for suspicion that Shakespeare might have expressed himself on the dread mystery in some such light-hearted manner as Echegaray. The Spanish dramatist, however, omits one important condition which he, at least, has well fulfilled. He has all through life acted up to the letter of Carlyle's teaching as to the "perennial nobleness and even sacredness" of "Work." With him the main necessity in all the ways of life is hard labour, untiring drill, constant self-perfection. In his own example he seems to declare that even poets cannot straightway claim to be in the charmed circle of Mascarille's "gens de qualité" qui "savent tout sans avoir jamais rien appris."

Perhaps one of the first things calculated to strike a student of Echegaray is the air of gloom which overhangs many of his graver dramas. Instances might be given in which a combination of nearly all the elements of woe and despair, frequently leads to a catastrophe, from the contemplation of which others besides the mere hysterical reader will find it difficult to turn away with calmness. Yet this writer may, in a certain sense, be said to have in him something of classic delicacy and reserve — with regard, in especial, to scenes of death. The introduction of death upon the stage seems invariably a matter of concern to him. Not that it is ever awkwardly shrunk from. Indeed, when used as a last resort, when "fear has had laid upon it as much as it can bear," "when life is weaned and wearied till it is ready to drop," then death in the hands of Echegaray comes forward at times with the weight of an almost overwhelming consummation. The Spanish dramatist, in short, may fairly claim a portion of that pleasing reverence for the dead which all true artists have. To adduce illustrations which must appear unfashionable in days when half a continent may be depopulated, without much protest, in the course of a single volume. The author of "Guy Mannering" and the author of "Monte Cristo," in the very height of the gaiety, the gallantry, the majesty of their descriptions of their own and former times; Dickens and Thackeray, in the full flow of their mocking indignation or their lacerating irony, will be seen all at once to stop short. Their looks change. Their tones become softened and their eyes downcast. They uncover their heads and compel us to do the same. For they have led us into the presence of the dead; and before the lowliest or the loftiest of their fellows — Meg Merrilies or the Abbé Faria, Betty Higden or Colonel Newcome — these rare spirits incline themselves in solemn veneration.

Of Echegaray's power over the pulses of sorrow and terror, without the intervention of death, an example may be found in "El Hijo de Don Juan." And here, perhaps, a few words may not be out of place, even in view of Echegaray's own "Prologue," as to the true source of this drama. That it was inspired by the reading of Ibsen's "Ghosts," we have the Spaniard's own declaration. But were it permissible to put aside the fact that both works treat of the problem of heredity in its most hideous and harrowing form, and the minor circumstance of the borrowing of

Oswald's phrase, "Mother, give me the sun!"—words which, to the mind of Echegaray, embody such picturesque and profound significance—Mr. William Archer himself might not be reluctant to admit the essential originality of the Spanish play. The truth is that "El Hijo de Don Juan" is a sombre and relentless satire upon the real national hero of Spain, the being immortalised by Molière and Mozart, and more or less caricatured in the cruder imagination of José Zorilla. Don Juan, the gamester, the libertine, the duellist, the bully, has been transported from the sixteenth century to the nineteenth. He is in entirely new surroundings and has become in a measure reformed. We find him past the sixtieth year of his age, with a wife whom he has indeed ill-treated, but with a son of whom he never tires of boasting. The disorders of his youth have left him with none the strongest of brains. And now the sins of the parent, in accordance with Echegaray's unsparing rule, are visited upon the child. The father's own mental weakness is developed in the most grim and terrible form in the gifted son. And so the flames in which Don Juan Tenorio was untimely plunged, are rekindled in the hell of misery and remorse with which the heir to his shameless renown sees the final overthrow of his boy's intellect. It is hardly too much to say that the "Ghosts" is almost bright and frolicsome in comparison with the "Son of Don Juan." Echegaray has here deliberately chosen colours of funereal blackness, and has laid them on with little regard for the feelings of the sensitive reader. Ibsen leads us to the edge of his own "Inferno," and points to the pale faces of those whom his genius has condemned to immortal suffering; but he hurries us aside before we have time to become giddy. Echegaray drags us pitilessly down and holds us fast, while in our very presence his victims are whirled shrieking past us—borne along on burning winds, or stretched in agony on the rack. Still with all deductions, the gift of true impressiveness, which has been so abundantly acknowledged in Ibsen, will scarcely be denied to the Spaniard who so frankly admits the influence of the Northern master. This impressiveness may be set down to pathological causes, to the unwholesomeness of the subject, to the lugubrious moral atmosphere in which a pessimist like Ibsen, a teacher of Hebraic sternness like Echegaray, loves at times to fold himself round. But whether the effect of plays of this kind may or may not be illegitimate, it is, perhaps, within its peculiar limits, entirely unexampled. Plays of high name, plays filled with scenes of violence, with the ring and storm of battle, with midnight murder, with death in its worst forms, might be placed for comparison beside the "Son of Don Juan." And though there is not a death, not a blow struck from beginning to end of the Spanish drama, such plays, with all their accumulations of misery and ferocity, might be found to yield in the element of sheer horror to the spectacle of the brilliant Lazarus, the poet, the dramatist, the coming glory of Spain, waking from a trance under the anguished eyes of his father, his mother, his betrothed, and bursting into the ravings of a hopeless madman.

Of Echegaray's use of dramatic resources when he indeed brings death upon the stage, a few examples may be quoted. In "El Gran Galeoto" the sudden exposure of the body of Julian to his unforgiven wife. In "Mariana" the bloody sacrifice of the heroine—in presence of her real lover—by the husband whom she loathes and defies. Lover and husband stand armed over the corpse; but the stage is not therefore converted into a shambles; we are merely left to conjecture that the two desperate men confronting each other will not long survive the woman who has coloured in such sinister fashion the lives of both. Another example, more openly verging on the melodramatic, may be encountered in an earlier drama than these, "En el seno de la Muerte." Here is one of the rare instances in which Echegaray has chosen a purely romantic period for the scene of his play. A husband, treacherously wronged by the brother and the wife whom he had almost equally loved, contrives his revenge. He locks himself and the two culprits in the family mausoleum, of which he alone has the key and he alone knows the secret. He does not ignore, they do not ignore, the fact that there is no escape for any one of them. After a painful scene of reproach, at the end of which the traitor brother kills himself, the husband first throws the key which had locked them in, then the torch which had illumined the dismal magnificence of their surroundings, down a deep cavity which yawns between the monuments. Finally, in utter darkness, he stabs himself dead at his wife's feet; and the curtain falls amidst an undefinable impression of haunting dismay at the alternatives of fate before the lonely survivor.

For obvious reasons Echegaray has been here referred to in connection with Ibsen. Whether an apology for such a conjunction of names might in reason be demanded by the most loyal of Ibsenites is doubtful, under the present conditions of criticism. It cannot but be a source of relief to any one helping to introduce a new author to the public, that the process of comparison has been simplified of late; that the qualifications exacted from competitors are drawn up in a spirit of charming leniency; that the certificate of immortality is made more than ever easy of attainment. Some years ago a writer thought fit, not only without seeming sense of shame, but with the complacent air of one who sees "a new planet swim into his ken," to couple the names of Mr. Rudyard Kipling and Charles Dickens. It must have been under the inspiration of such criticism as this that Shakespeare was immediately dethroned—for at least the hundredth time—and once again at the hands of "our lively neighbour the Gaul." Corneille, Racine, and Victor Hugo were allowed to slumber tranquilly in their graves, and it was admitted on behalf of England—by the Paris *Figaro*—that the author of "Othello" was surpassed by M. Maurice Maeterlinck. Even under these encouraging circumstances, however, it will not be here contended that Señor Echegaray shows in his work anything comparable—"et oserai-je le dire," as M. Mirbeau would say—"supérieure en beauté à ce qu'il y a de plus beau dans Shakespeare." It might be suggested that "Mariana"—Señor Echegaray's masterpiece in female creation—would have been readily accepted as a companion with Charmian and Iras in attendance on the most complex of all heroines —Cleopatra. Further than this it will not be safe to go.

Echegaray may be noted as displaying, even in the following mournful drama, a genuine and, as a rule, unforced sense of humour. In his comic passages, however, he has a fault which he shares with Shakespeare—and the editor of *Punch*. He is a remorseless punster.

This poet's genius, as may have been remarked, burst into bloom at a time beyond the midsummer of life. He was forty-two before his first drama was produced.

That is twenty-one years ago. Since then his activity has never known exhaustion. He is now the author of some fifty plays. There are particular years among the past twenty-one in the course of which he has put upon the stage as many as four dramas, not one of which is carelessly written, though one imitation from the German, "El Gladiador de Ravena," was commenced and completed within three days. During these twenty-one years, indeed, he appears to have determined on making up for what, in other important respects, had certainly not been lost time. Civil engineers have found and still find it to their advantage to consult him on points which are the special study and occupation of their lives. He has published three formidable volumes on the "Modern Theories of Physics." A well-known book of his has appeared on sub-marine vessels of war. He has lectured on Political Economy and Geology with equal success. He is admitted by Spaniards to be the chief of their own mathematicians; they further claim for him the honour of being one of the first mathematicians in the world. He is an orator who has won the applause of Castelar himself. There were only wanting his labours as a poet and a dramatist to set the seal upon a career of almost universal aptitude. Those labours have earned for him a renown which will assuredly not be allowed to die in his own country.

Be the praise high or low, in view of the condition of Spanish literature between the seventeenth century and the nineteenth, Spaniards declare that for more than two hundred years their drama has not brought forth a serious rival to this man. And there can hardly be a doubt that, in any selection of names of the greatest dramatists ever sprung from Spain, Lope de Vega and Calderon de la Barca will find the place nearest to themselves occupied by José Echegaray.

TWO WORDS BY WAY OF PROLOGUE.

IN trying to interpret the idea of my last drama, "The Son of Don Juan," the critics have said many things. That the idea was the same as that which inspired Ibsen in his celebrated work entitled "Gengangere." That the passions which it sets in movement are more natural to the countries of the North than to our sunnier climes : that it deals with the problem of hereditary lunacy. That it discusses the law of heredity. That it is sombre and lugubrious, with no other object than that of arousing horror. That it is a purely pathological drama. That it contains nothing more than the progress of a case of lunacy. That from the moment when it is perceived that Lazarus will go mad, the interest of the work ceases, and nothing remains but to follow step by step the shipwreck of the poor creature—and so forth. I think that all this is but a series of lamentable equivocations on the part of the great and little judges of the dramatic art. The idea of my drama was not one of those mentioned. Its motive is very different, but I shall not explain it. Why should I? In all the scenes of my work, in all its personages, in nearly all its phrases it is explained. Moreover, to explain it would be dangerous; it might be imagined that my proposal was to defend the poor Son of Don Juan under the pretext of exposing the central idea from which he drew birth. I never defend my dramas; when I write their last word I leave them to their fate. I neither defend them materially nor morally. I finish a drama, I give it to the management of a theatre, it is put on the stage, it is liked or not liked, according to the favour of God. The management does what is most suited to its interests, without my interference: the actors represent it as they can, almost always very well, the public pronounces its judgment in one sense or another, according to its feelings, and the critics unbosom themselves to their satisfaction. I neither wish nor ought, if only from good taste, to defend my new drama; but it contains one phrase which *is not mine*, which *is Ibsen's*; and that phrase I must defend energetically, for I consider it one of extraordinary beauty: " Mother, give me the sun," says Lazarus. And this phrase, simple, infantile, almost comic, enfolds a world of ideas, an ocean of sentiments, a hell of sorrows, a cruel lesson, a supreme warning to society and to the family circle. Thus I look at it. A generation devoured by vice; which bears even in its bones the virus engendered by impure love; with a corrupted blood which in its course drags along organisms of corruption mingled with its ruddy globules, this generation goes on falling and falling into the abysses of idiocy: the cry of Lazarus is the last twilight of a reason which founders in the eternal blackness of imbecility. And at the same time nature awakes and the sun comes forth—another twilight which will very soon be all light. And the two twilights meet and cross and salute each other with the salutation of everlasting farewell at the close of the drama.

Reason, which is precipitated downward, impelled by the corruption of pleasure. The sun, which springs upward with immortal flames, impelled by the sublime forces of nature. Below, human reason which has come to an end; above, the sun which begins a new day. "Give me the sun," says Lazarus to his mother. Don Juan likewise asked for it from between the tresses of the woman of Tarifa. On this point there is much to be said: it gives room for much thought. For, in truth, if our society. . . . But what the devil are these philosophical speculations that I am plunging into? Let every man compose such for himself as best he may, and let him clamour for the sun or beg for the horns of the moon, or ask for what suits his appetite. Does nobody understand or take an interest in these matters? What then? This, at most would prove that the modern Don Juan continues to bequeath many sons to the world, though they have not the talent of Lazarus. Let us give a respectful greeting to the sons of Don Juan.

JOSÉ ECHEGARAY.

PERSONS OF THE DRAMA.

CARMEN.
DONA DOLORES.
PACA.
TERESA.
LAZARUS.
DON JUAN.
DON TIMOTEO.
DOCTOR BERMUDEZ.
JAVIER.
DON NEMESIO.

First represented March 29, 1892.

[*Rights of adaptation and stage representation reserved.*]

ACT I.

The scene represents a room for business or study. It is mounted in <u>elegant yet severe taste</u>, with something of a worldly style, indicated by some artistic object which betrays predilections of that kind. On the left of the spectator is a <u>very light and charming tea-table</u> to accommodate three or four persons; upon the table is a candle or night-light with a <u>bright-coloured shade</u>; and surrounding it are three small arm-chairs or cushioned seats and smoking chairs. On the right is a desk—not very large, though massive and sober in style: behind, a chair or writing stool. At the side of the desk a high stool or better still an arm-chair. Upon the desk a lighted lamp with a dark shade. Also on the desk, in a framed easel, the photograph of CARMEN. *On the left first wing <u>a balcony</u>, to the <u>right a fireplace with</u> a very bright fire: at one side a large portative screen. Over the doors and the balcony <u>thick, sober-hued curtains</u>. A door in the background, and a door at either side. If it be possible, there should also be in the background a <u>small bookcase, dark and rich</u>: at the left forming a <u>pendant</u>, a cabinet, <u>dark like the bookcase</u>, and full of objects of art. If this be impossible, two equivalent pieces of furniture. In short, a room which gives evidence of rich though* *not opulent possessors, and which above all denotes the contrast of two tastes:—the one austere, the other gay and worldly. It is night.*

SCENE.

Don Juan, *and* Don Timoteo, Don Nemesio *discovered seated round the tea-table, drinking strong liqueurs and smoking. The three are old, but give token of different types: the three bear the stamp of life-long self-indulgence. It is recognised, however, that* Don Juan *has been a man of gaiety and fashion.*

Juan. Timoteo!
Tim. What?
Juan. I have a suspicion.
Tim. What about?
Juan. That we are getting old.
Tim. How have you got to know?
Juan. I'll tell you: there are symptoms. When the weather changes all my joints are sore. When I wish to stretch out this leg merrily, it entails labour on me, and in the end it is the other leg which moves. Moreover my sight is failing: when I see a dark girl in the street, she looks fair to me; and if a girl happens to be fair, she becomes so obscured as to turn dark before my eyes.
Nem. That's weakness; you should take a tonic. (*Drinks.*)
Juan. My stomach cannot endure alcohol now: I drink out of compliment; but I know that it does me harm.
Tim. Because it is not the alcohol of our time.

NEM. This is corrosive sublimate alcoholised.

TIM. It is the alcohol which has grown old. (*Walks about jauntily.*) I feel young still—Ah !

JUAN. What's the matter?

TIM. While simply moving I seem to have disjointed my whole vertebral column. The devil, the devil !

NEM. (*drinking calmly*). Something or other will have got dislocated.

JUAN. Let us undeceive ourselves: we are nearing the City of Old Age. By the life of life, how short is life ! (*Strikes the chair with his fist.*) Ah !

TIM. What ails you?

JUAN. A pain in the elbow—and in this shoulder.

NEM. The weather; it's damp. (*Drinks.*)

TIM. Juanito, you have never been very strong.

JUAN. I have not been? I have not been? I have been stronger than you all. For twenty-four hours running I have played cards: for three days running I have been shut up with Pacorro and Luis emptying bottles: and my patron Saint Juan Tenorio, from the heaven where he dwells in company with Doña Inez, will have seen how I have borne myself in amorous enterprises. You, on the other hand, have been nothing more than the braggadocios of vice. Away with such lay-figures.

TIM. We don't deny that you have been a greater madcap than anybody else; but strong—what's called a strong man—that you have not been.

NEM. You have not been that—confess.

JUAN. What have I to confess?

TIM. Something has happened to you which never happened to any one else.

JUAN. What happened to me?

TIM. In order to get your spine straightened you

had to be put in a casing of paste, and they used to hang you up by the neck twice a day.

JUAN. But that was because we were playing at single stick in the Plaza de Toros, and they broke two of my ribs; that might happen to anybody.

TIM. No, no: you were not like us. Do you remember, Nemesio? "Where is Juanito?" "In bed." "Where is Juanito?" "At Panticosa." "Where is Juanito?" "At Archena." "Where is Juanito?" "Shut up in his casing." "Where is Juanito?" "At this moment they must be hanging him." Ha, ha!

TIM. and NEM. laugh. DON JUAN looks at them angrily.

JUAN. Don't laugh very loud, or we shall have a general breaking up. I have been a man and you two have been pitiful fellows. You (*to* TIM.), got married at forty: you locked yourself up in a corner of this town with your wife, and there was an end of Timoteo. You (*to* NEM.), flying like a coward from the storms of the world, took refuge in Arganda, where you drink each year the vintage of the year before. I, on the other hand (*speaking with proud emphasis*), I—it is true that I also got married—at forty-two; but that's no proof of weakness. If Don Juan Tenorio had been allowed the time, he would have married Doña Inez, and indeed there is a rumour that they celebrated their mystic wedding in heaven. But I, the other Don Juan, got married like a man, like a free citizen; yet I did not thereupon abandon the field of honour. I am myself at home, myself abroad, at nine in the convent, at ten in this street. Well, then I had my Lazarus!—Eh!—There's a lad! That's what it is to have a son.

TIM. God help me, with your glorious triumph! Jump into the street, and you won't see a neighbour who is not the son of somebody. Each individual has a father.

NEM. One father at least.

JUAN. Yes, but I was the libertine; I was the man that drained the cup of pleasure and the cask from the wine-cellar: the invalid of the orgie. "That fellow is consumptive," they used to say. "That fellow will die some morning," you thought. And suddenly I became restored to life in Lazarus. Lazarus is my resurrection. And how robust and strong he is. And what talent he has! A prodigy—a Byron, an Espronceda, an Edgar Poe—a genius. That's not what I alone say: you have it written in all the journals of Madrid.

TIM. Yes, the lad is able.

NEM. He is able.

JUAN. Well, now, frankly—he who has led the life that I have led—he who while saying: "I must rest for a time," has a son like Lazarus: that man—is he not a man, indeed?

TIM. Fine subject of rejoicing for a Tenorio.

JUAN. What subject?

TIM. This of yours. Does it not come to this that you are the father of a genius?

JUAN. And what then, dotards? Strength is strength, and becomes transformed: you don't understand this. I make no doubt that I had all the genius of Lazarus concealed in some corner of my brain; but as I gave it neither time nor opportunity it could not exhibit itself. At last it grew tired of waiting, and it said: "Eh! I am going with the son, because with the father I can make no headway." (*Laughing.*)

Tim. Don't delude yourself, Juanito. The talent of Lazarus, for indeed he seems to have great talent, is not inherited from you: he must have derived it from his mother. (The paternal heritage will have been some rheumatism, some affection of the nerves.

Nem. The sediments of pleasure and the dregs of alcohol. (*Drinks.*)

Juan. Blockheads! I went through my school-days badly, and I lived worse; but there was something in me.

Tim. Quite a genius frittered away on a lost soul.

Juan. It may be so.

Nem. And by what did you recognise this something?

Tim. When was it?

Nem. And where?

Juan. It was on awaking from a drunken bout.

Tim. Now that you are going to ascend to the sublime don't say a drunken bout.

Juan. Well then, on arising from an orgie.

Nem. That's well. "To Jarifa in an Orgie," Espronceda. (*Drinks.*)

Juan. Yes, senor, the very thing. I once felt that which neither of you ever experienced.

Nem. Tell us, tell us. This ought to be curious. Another little glass, Timoteo.

Tim. Come. To the health of the disappointed genius. (*Coughing.*)

Nem. Of the unsuccessful genius. (*Drinks.*)

Don Juan *is thoughtful.*

Tim. Begin.

Juan. You remember the season we passed at my country seat in Sevilla, in the year—in the year——?

TIM. The year I don't recollect—but very well do I remember the country-house, on the banks of the Guadalquivir, with an Oriental saloon, divans, carpets—those famous carpets.

NEM. True, true! I was always walking on them. Aniceta, the little gipsy—you remember?—used to cry out, "I am sinking, I am sinking."

TIM. True, true! and as she was so little she used to sink out of sight, really.

NEM. Delightful time. Don Juan's country seat—so we called it.

TIM. What I liked was that running balcony or gallery, or whatever it was. What a view! The Guadalquivir! And it looked towards the East—<u>you saw the sun rise</u>—it was enchanting. (*To* JUAN.) Have you fallen asleep?

JUAN. I? I never sleep. That's what I should like—to sleep. For this is the way I pass the night—with a wrench of this nerve and a wrench at the other. The little pain which is in the neighbourhood of my elbow goes for a walk. My cough appears before it and says, "Good evening, neighbour." My head cries out, "I am going to waltz for a while, stand away there." And my stomach heaves, "No, for God's sake; I shall be sea-sick." Sleep, indeed! It's ten years since I have slept.

NEM. But you are not telling us the story.

JUAN. What story?

TIM. Why, man, that about the fiery outbreak of genius. When you learned that you had something inside here. (*Touching his forehead.*) Something sublime, eh?

NEM. I should think so, corrosive sublimate. Ha, ha! Another little glass.

TIM. Come. However, we are left at where you

got to know once upon a time that you were a larva-like genius—like the pulmonary larvæ.

JUAN. I got to know it. There's nothing to laugh at.

NEM. In your country seat by the Guadalquivir?

JUAN. The very same.

TIM. In the Oriental saloon—the one with the divans, the balcony looking towards the East and the Persian carpet?

JUAN. Exactly.

TIM. During a night of orgies?

JUAN. No—next morning—on awaking.

TIM. On awaking from the orgie! "Bring hither, Jarifa, bring hither thine hand—come and place it upon my brow!" (*Taking the hand of* DON NEMESIO.)

NEM. (*withdrawing his hand*). Your brow is all right. Ha, ha! Don't make me laugh.

TIM. Then look—thine hand—a pure branch of the vine.

JUAN. Don't you want to hear me?

NEM. I should think so. Tell your story.

TIM. But you must tell it seriously, solemnly, dramatically. The awaking of Don Juan—after a night of orgies.

JUAN. Then here goes.

NEM. *and* TIM. *take convenient positions for listening to him.*

It was a grand night—a grand supper. There were eight of us—each with a partner. Everybody was drunk—even the Guadalquivir. Aniceta appeared on the gallery and began to cry out, "Stupid, insipid, waterish river, drink wine for once!" and she threw a bottle of Manzanilla into it.

TIM. She was very lively, Aniceta. She once

threw a bottle of wine at my head—but it was empty.

NEM. Your head?

TIM. The bottle. Continue, continue — but, seriously—eh?

JUAN. Well, I was lying asleep along the floor, upon the carpet, close to a divan. And on the divan there had fallen by one of the usual accidents, the Tarifena—Paca, the Tarifena. Nobody noticed it, and on the divan she lay asleep. Amidst her tossings to and fro, her hair had become loose—a huge mass! and it fell over me in silky waves—a great quantity.

NEM. Not like Timoteo's. (TIMOTEO *is bald.*)

JUAN. Not like Timoteo's. But if you interrupt me I shall lose the inspiration.

TIM. Continue—continue, seriously, Juanito.

JUAN. We leave off at where I was asleep on the carpet, when the loosened hair of the Tarifena fell over my head and face, enfolding me as in a splendid black mantle of perfumed lace. Would you like anything more serious?

TIM. It goes well so.

NEM. Keep yourself to that height.

TIM. To the height of the carpet?

NEM. Each one mounts to the height of which he is worthy. Go on.

JUAN. The dawn arrived. It was summer.

TIM. And yet it rained.

JUAN. No, my dear fellow, a delightful morning: the balcony open: the East with splendid curtains of mist and of little red clouds, the sky blue and stainless, a light more vivid kindling into flame the distant horizon.

TIM. So, so—to that height.

Nem. Very poetical, very poetical—don't fall off.

Juan. Slowly the crimson globe ascended. I opened my eyes wide, and I saw the sun. I saw it from between the interwoven tresses of the Tarifena—it inundated me with its light, and I stretched forth my hand instinctively to grasp it. Something of a new kind of love, a new desire agitated me. Great brightness, much azure, very broad spheres, vague yet burning aspirations—for something very beautiful. For a minute I understood that there is something higher than the pleasure of the senses: for a minute I felt myself another being. I wafted a kiss to the sun, and pulled aside in anger the girl's hair. One lock clung about my lips—it touched my palate and gave me nausea. I flung away the tress—I awoke the Tarifena—and vice dawned through the remains of the orgie, like the sun through the vapours of the night, its mists and its fire-coloured clouds.

Tim. Good for Juanito. We are moved, profoundly moved.

Nem. Unfathomably-moved. (*Drinks.*)

Tim. But with what object have you told us all that I don't remember.

Juan. To prove to you that there have existed within me noble aspirations.

Tim. Ah! yes, sublime desires.

Nem. Superhuman longings.

Juan. Quite so: and that everything which was deprived of the opportunity of making itself known in me, or which ran to waste through other channels will revive in my Lazarus in the forms of talent, inspiration, genius, wings that flutter, creations that spring forth, applause, glory, immorality. Ah! you'll see—you'll see.

Tim. Your posthumous blowing off of steam.

JUAN. My last and most pure illusion—no, the only pure illusion of my existence. And you ought to be glad that my son is getting on so well, you scapegrace. (*Giving* TIM. *a playful slap.*)

TIM. I?

NEM. Ah, ah! I understand you. Another glass to the health of the bride and bridegroom.

JUAN. Eh? What do you say? (*To* DON T.)

TIM. Ah, yes; no, it is impossible. My poor Carmen is very much in love: but I don't know if Lazarus——

JUAN. Lazarus is mad about her. He is reserved enough, but he is mad.

TIM. Well, look; if the son is going to resemble the papa I should be very sorry to form the relationship, frankly.

JUAN. Much obliged to you, venerable grandfather.

NEM. No, Lazarus is very steady.

TIM. The fact is that my girl is very weak, very delicate, a sensitive plant. Her poor chest troubles her with the least thing; and if Lazarus were to lead my poor Carmen the life which you have led your wife, I should renounce the relationship and the honour which you propose to me.

JUAN. Gently, gently; I have been an irreproachable husband.

TIM. Oh!

NEM. Ah!

JUAN. Irreproachable. My wife has always been first in my affections.

TIM. But you have had a second, and a third——

NEM. And a fourth and a fifth.

JUAN. Those are lawful requirements of the system of numeration.

NEM. Peace between the future fathers-in-law. The

one is as good as the other; the one is just as gay as the other; and one is quite as sedate a father of a family as the other.

JUAN. And of course you must be better than we are! You who have been steeped in alcohol from your tenderest years.

NEM. Between the bottle and the woman, I cling to the bottle.

TIM. Well, I to the woman.

JUAN. Let us not exaggerate: being between the bottle and the woman one remains just the same—between the bottle and the woman.

TIM. Not quite: we now remain at home between our own woman and the bottle of tisan—two tisans.

NEM. Because you are a pair of dotards. I am every night at the theatre, in my little box: from ten to twelve I consecrate myself to art. Some dancers have come from Madrid. Sweet zephyrs! Four zephyrs!

JUAN (*in a loud voice and erecting himself like an old cock*). Are they pretty?

TIM. Your wife will hear you.

JUAN (*lowering his voice in exaggerated style*). Are they pretty?

NEM. Four flowers, four stars, four goddesses, the four cardinal points of beauty. What eyes! What waists! What vigour! What cushion-like bodies.

JUAN. Cushion-like?

NEM. Nothing artificial.

JUAN. Nothing artificial? And you are going to the theatre now?

NEM. I go there to finish the night as God commands—in admiring the marvels of creation. (*Rising.*)

TIM. Then I'll accompany you, and we shall both admire them. (*Rising.*)

JUAN. Well, I'll not stay at home. I'll go there with you two and we shall all three admire them. (*Rising with difficulty.*)

NEM. At this time of night, Juanito?

JUAN. You two are going at this time of night.

TIM. And what will your wife say?

JUAN. For twenty-five years my wife has said nothing. Besides, I give orders here. No one ever calls me to account. Ho, there, I'll be back in a moment. Ho, there! [*Exit.*

NEM. I think that poor Juan is getting to the end of his tether. Don't you see how he walks? What things he says! What pitiful senilities!

TIM. Yet he is not very old.

NEM. What should make him old? He is little more than sixty. Every man who respects himself is sixty years old. (*Walking about somewhat jauntily.*)

TIM. Precisely: you are sixty, I am sixty, every well-conditioned person is sixty.

NEM. But he has lived! What a life he has lived! This is what I say: people may be guilty of follies: you have been guilty of them: I have been guilty of them——

TIM. And every well-behaved person is guilty of them.

NEM. But up to a certain point.

TIM. Up to a certain point.

NEM. But poor Juan was old at forty. And Lazarus is not what his father says—no, señor.

TIM. Well, talent—he has much talent. All the newspapers of Madrid assert it; you see it now. That he is a prodigy that he will be a glory to the nation.

NEM. I don't deny it. But walk with care before marrying little Carmen to him.

TIM. Why? The devil! Why? Is he like his father?

NEM. No! Like the father—no. Inclined to gaiety—yes. What would you have the son of Don Juan to be?

TIM. Everybody is inclined to gaiety. I am so, you are so——

NEM. It is not that. It is that according to my information (*lowering his voice*) he is not so robust as the papa supposes. Lazarus suffers from vertigo—nervous attacks—what shall I say?—something of that sort. At long intervals, it's true; but that head of his is not strong. That's why he does such stupendous things, and that's why they call him a genius. Don't trust men of genius, Timoteo. A genius goes along the street, and every one says, "The genius! the genius!" He turns round the corner, and the little boys in the next street run after him shouting: "The madman! the madman!" Timoteo, it is very dangerous to have much cleverness.

TIM. God deliver us from it. Oh! as to that I have always been very careful.

NEM. So have I. A man should not be altogether a fool; that's not well. But the thing is—don't be a genius.

TIM. Never. Here's Juan coming back.

NEM. Say nothing to him of what I have told you. They either don't know of the sufferings of Lazarus, or they hide them; it's natural.

TIM. Not a word! but it's well to know it.

Re-enter DON JUAN.

JUAN (*dressed for going out*). Are we ready?

TIM. We are.

JUAN. Then let's march. Listen. (*To* TIM.) Will you come back for Carmen, or must we take her?

TIM. Carmen?

JUAN. Yes, Carmen. Have you already forgotten that she is in there with Dolores?

TIM. It's true.

JUAN. What a head! Ha, ha! And you say that I——? He forgets his own daughter! It would have been easy for me to forget my Lazarus. What a fellow you are! What a fellow you are! Away with you for a pair of wooden-heads! (*Laughing.*)

TIM. You gay young dog, lead us on to glory and to pleasure!

JUAN. I shall lead you on to the cemetery if you annoy me any more. However, what do you decide? Will you come back to fetch Carmen?

TIM. I shall have to come back to carry you home.

JUAN. You carry me? You'd never be able to carry any one.

NEM. I shall carry you both. Come, give me your arm, Juanito. If not you can't go down the staircase. (DON JUAN *takes his arm.*)

JUAN. Teresa—little Teresa.

TERESA *enters from the back centre.*

TER. Señor?

JUAN. Tell Dolores—tell your mistress—that I am going out. Let Señorita Carmen wait until her father returns to fetch her. March on. (*To* TIM.) Take hold of me, for you are not very strong. Take hold of me.

TIM. March on.

NEM. March on.

JUAN. Military step! One—two—

TIM. (*looking at* TERESA). This girl's prettier every day.

NEM. (*the same*). And fresher.

JUAN (*to* NEM). You are not looking; you will fall.

TER. Where are you going, señor?

JUAN. To take these two to the lunatic asylum.

[*Exeunt laughing and clutching each other's arms.*

TER. (*looking from the back*). Well, when you get in there, may they never let you out. Where are those mummies going?

Enter DONA DOLORES *and* CARMEN *from the right.*

CAR. Ah! They are not here. Papa is not here.

DOL. Have they gone out?

TER. Yes, señora. But Don Juan left word that Señorita Carmen's papa would come back to take her home.

CARMEN *coughs.*

DOL. Coughing again! You ought not to go out at night; the doctor has forbidden you. You don't take care of yourself. You are a little simpleton. Sick children should be in their little homes.

CAR. When I am alone I am very sad. I had rather cough than be sad.

DOL. Not so; I shall go and bear you company. And I shall bring Lazarus. I don't wish my sick child, my darling child to be melancholy. (*Fondling her.*)

CARMEN *coughs.*

Again!

CAR. It's not worth speaking of.

DOL. The fact is that no one can breathe here. What an atmosphere! What smoke! What a smell of tobacco.

TER. The three ancient gentlemen were all the night drinking and smoking and laughing. Now you see how they have left everything.

DOL. Yes, I see. (*Looking with disgust at the*

little table which is full of ashes and ends of cigars and covered with bottles, glasses, and waiters' trays.) Take these things away; clean everything up; open the balcony. I am not accustomed—yet after twenty-five years I should have grown accustomed. (*Aside.*) The poetry of existence! (*Laughing bitterly.*)

CAR. What are you laughing at, Dolores?

DOL. (*changing her tone and feigning merriment*). I feel amused, very much amused at the frolics of those three venerable old men.

CAR. Papa is not yet an old man.

DOL. He is not: but what a life he has led. (*Recollecting herself.*) So laborious—his business—his commerce—the same as Juan.

CAR. Ah yes. Parents are all alike, killing themselves for their children. And papa is very good. He loves me—my God! At night he gets up I don't know how many times and listens at the door of my room to know if I am coughing, so that I, who hear him, stifle the cough with my handkerchief or with the bed-clothes; but sometimes I am not able—it is that I am choking. (*Coughs.*)

DOL. (*to* TERESA *who has been meanwhile taking away bottles, ash-trays, waiters' trays, and who has entered and gone out several times*). Open the balcony! Let in the fresh, pure air. No, wait. (*To* CARMEN.) You could not bear the sensation, my poor little one. Come. (*Taking her by the hand.*)

CAR. Where to?

DOL. While the room is being ventilated you must remain like a quiet little girl behind this curtain. (*Placing her behind the curtain to the right.*) A quiet little girl, eh? Afterwards you shall enter.

CAR. (*laughing*). Are you leaving me in punishment?

Dol. In punishment! Your father is very indulgent, I am very severe.

Car. Good; but your punishment does not last long.

Dol. Not very long. (*To* Teresa.) Go: I shall open it. [*Exit* Teresa.

Dolores *opens the balcony*.

So! Air—the air of night—space—freshness—that which is pure—that which is great—that which does not revolt one—that which dilates the lungs—that which expands the soul! To have a very broad horizon which one may fill with hopes, and to run towards those hopes! At least hope! Hope! Oh! I cannot complain. I have my Lazarus—then I have everything.

Car. (*putting her head from time to time through the curtain*). May I come out?

Dol. No, not yet; wait—quiet, my little one. (*Walking from the balcony to the fireplace.*) To have my son! But without him ever having had a father—above all, that father! Oh, if my Lazarus had sprung spontaneously from my love! Even as—as the wave of the sea or the light of the sun springs forth. After all, let me not complain—even if he resembled—though he does not resemble—his father, Lazarus is mine and mine only. How good! How noble. What intellect! What a heart! Oh, what it is to have such a son!

Car. May I come in?

Dol. Ah, yes—wait though—I shall first shut the balcony. (*Shuts it.*) Come in.

Car. That's very different. (*Breathing with pleasure.*)

Dol. You feel well?

CAR. Very well.

DOL. What are you looking at?

CAR. The clock—to see what time it is. It is getting late: Lazarus is not coming. (*Sadly*.)

DOL. It is not late, my child. Come and sit by me.

CAR. Yes, it is late, it is late.

DOL. Lazarus will come soon. He knew that you were coming this evening, and he will not fail.

CAR. (*sorrowfully*). But he would do wrong to inconvenience himself for me. If he does not see me now, he'll see me another day.

DOL. You silly child, are you complaining?

CAR. Not at all. My God! He has his engagements, and he must not sacrifice himself for Carmen.

DOL. Carmen deserves it all; and Carmen knows it; don't be a little hypocrite.

CAR. No, señora, I speak as I think, and that's what gives me much pain and makes me quick at finding fault. You fondle me and love me, as if you were my own mother, now that I no longer have one. You watch over our love—the love of Lazarus and myself. I am sure you tell Lazarus that I am this and that—in short, a prodigy. And you swear to me that Lazarus is mad for the love of his Carmen. But is all this true? Can it be so? Am I worthy of Lazarus? Can such a man as he feel the passion which you describe to me for a poor creature like myself?

DOL. Come, now—I shall get vexed. Don't say such things. Why, have you never looked into the glass?

CAR. Yes, many times—every day.

DOL. And what does the glass tell you?

CAR. That I am very pale, that I am very thin,

that I have very sad eyes, and that I rather resemble a mother of sorrows than a girl of eighteen. That's what it tells me, and it causes me a rather unpleasant feeling.

DOL. There are very malevolent mirrors, and yours is one of them. (*In a comic tone.*) They take the form of boats to give us long faces; they get blurred to make us pale; they become stained to sow freckles all over our skins; and they commit every kind of wickedness. Yours is a criminal looking-glass; I'll send you one in which you may see what you are, and you shall see an angel gazing through a tiny window of crystal.

CAR. Yes. (*Laughs.*) But even if I were the most beautiful woman in the world, could I be worthy of Lazarus? A man like him!—A future such as his! A talent which all admire. Nay, a superior being. I love him much; but it makes me afraid and ashamed that he should know that I love him so much. I feel as if he were going to say to me: "But who are you, you little simpleton? Have you imagined that I am meant for an unsubstantial, ignorant, sickly little thing like you?" (*Sadly and humbly.*)

DOL. Well, Carmen, if you don't wish to make me angry, you will not talk such folly. A good woman is worth more than all the learned men of all the Academies. And if, as well as being good, she is pretty, then—then there's an end, there is no man who is worthy of her. Men, with the exception of Lazarus, are either mean-spirited wretches or heartless devils. (*In a rancorous tone.*)

CAR. Well, papa is very good, and is very fond of me.

DOL. Ah, yes—a very good person. But, if he had been so fond of you, he would have done better to give you stronger lungs.

Car. But, poor man, how is he to blame? If God did not wish——

Dol. Ah! yes, that's true. It is not Don Timoteo's fault. It was God's disposition that Carmen should have no more breathing powers than those of a little pigeon, and we must be resigned.

Car. Well, that's what I say. But Lazarus is not coming. You'll see that I shall have to go away before he comes. And, if he comes and sets to work, I shall be as little likely to see him to-night.

Dol. No; he has not written for some days. The excess of work has fatigued him. This constant thought is very wasting.

Car. But is he ill? (*With great anxiety.*)

Dol. No, child; fatigue, and nothing more.

Car. Yes; he is ill. I noticed that he was sad, preoccupied, but I thought, " There, it is that he does not love me, and he does not know how to tell me so."

Dol. What things you imagine! Neither the one nor the other. My Lazarus ill! Do you think that if he had been so I would not have set in motion all the first medical faculty here, and in Madrid, and in foreign parts? In any way, however (*somewhat uneasily*), you are right; he is very late.

Car. Did he go to the theatre?

Dol. No, to dine with some friends.

Car. Did Javier go?

Dol. He went also.

Car. I am glad; Javier is very sensible.

Dol. So is Lazarus.

Car. I should think so; but a good friend is never superfluous, and Javier has admiration, affection, and respect for Lazarus.

Dol. (*walking about impatiently*). Still, it is getting late—very late.

CARMEN *turns towards the balcony.*

What are you going to do?

CAR. Well, to watch and see if Lazarus is coming.

DOL. (*drawing her away from the balcony*). No, child ; you don't think of your poor chest, nor of that most obstinate cough of yours. Moreover, the night is very dark, and you could see nothing. Come away, Carmen, come away ; I'll watch.

CAR. If I can't see, neither will you see——

DOL. I shall try.

CAR. Wait ; I think he is coming, and with Javier.

DOL. (*listening*). Yes—it's true.

CAR. Are they not coming in here?

DOL. No ; they have gone straight to the room of Lazarus. But don't be uneasy ; as soon as he knows that you are here, he will come to see you.

CAR. Without doubt he comes back thinking of some great scene for his drama, or of some chapter of that book which he is writing and which they say is going to be a miracle of genius, or of some very intricate problem. Ah ! my God, whatever you may say, a man such as he cannot concern himself very much about an insignificant girl like myself.

DOL. Again !

CAR. I know nothing, I am worth nothing, I am nothing. I ? What am I fit for? Tell me. To stare at him like a blockhead while he is considering these great matters ; to watch at the balcony and see if he is coming, although it may be cold, and Carmen coughs incessantly ; to weep if he takes no notice of me, or if they tell me that he is ill. There is no doubt that little Carmen is capable of doing wonders. To look at him, to wait for him, to weep for him.

DOL. And what more can a woman do for a man ?

To look at him always, to wait for him always, to weep for him always.

CAR. And is that enough?

DOL. So much the worse for Lazarus if that should not be enough for him. But wait; he's here now; did I not tell you? as soon as he knew you were here.

CAR. (*joyfully*). It's true. How good he is.

Enter JAVIER.

JAV. A pleasant evening, Doña Dolores; pleasant evening, Carmen.

DOL. A very good evening.

CAR. And a very pleasant—but—Lazarus——

DOL. Is not Lazarus coming?

CAR. Is he ill?

DOL. Ah! if he is ill, I must go there——

JAV. (*stopping her*). No, for God's sake! What should make him ill? Listen to me. We and several friends have been dining with two writers from Madrid—people of our profession. We spoke of arts, of sciences, of politics, of philosophy, and of everything divine and human. We drank, we gave toasts, we made speeches, we read verses. You understand? And these things excite in an extraordinary way the nervous system of Lazarus.

DOL. And has anything gone wrong with him? My God!

CAR. Go, Dolores—go!

JAV. For the sake of God in heaven, let me conclude. These things, I say, shake his nerves, and his imagination becomes on fire; it soon discovers luminous horizons; the ideas rush upon him precipitately. Could you take upon yourselves the burden of them? No; that which came with the fever of inspiration he wished to take advantage of, and for that reason—

precisely for that reason—he locked himself up in his room and sent me away.

CAR. (*sadly to* DOLORES). Did I not say so? He would come—and to work.

DOL. Does he not know that Carmen is here?

JAV. They told us that on our entrance; but he pays attention to nothing, to nobody, when inspiration and glory and art cry aloud to him, "Come, we are waiting for you."

DOL. However—— (*Wishing to go.*)

CAR. No, for God's sake! (*Stopping her.*) He must be allowed to work. If through me he should lose any of those grand ideas which now hover fondly about him, what pain and what remorse for me! Disturb him that he may come and speak to me? No, not so; I am not so selfish. I asked for nothing better. By no means can I consent. (*Embraces* DOLORES; *coughs and almost weeps.*)

DOL. (*with anxiety*). What's the matter with you?

CAR. (*affecting merriment*). Nothing; it is only that I had begun to laugh and cough at the same time. I laughed because I was reminded of a tale—a very silly tale, which made me laugh, however, and which fits the case. You shall judge. There was a very sprightly little female donkey, which became enamoured of a most beautiful genius, who bore on his forehead a very red little flame, and had very white wings; and the bright genius, out of pure compassion, fondled the ears of the little donkey; and she, in accordance with her nature, began to leap for joy, and it overthrew the genius, clipped his wings, and he could fly no more. The blue of the firmament was cut off from the genius, and there was left to him nothing more than a very green meadow, a little female donkey who was very good, but who was, after all, a donkey. No, mother, I don't wish to be *the heroine of the story*. Let us allow the genius to fly.

DOL. (*to* JAVIER). See what a creature she is!

JAV. A criminal humility.

DOL. But, indeed, if you persist, we shall let him work.

CAR. Don't you think we might let him have this room free to himself? Here he has his books of predilection, and he has more room, and he can walk about; he has told me many times that he composes verses while walking about.

DOL. A good idea! Let us go to my sitting-room. (*To* JAVIER.) Tell him that we abandoned the field to him, and that he may come without fear.

JAV. (*laughing*). Noble sacrifice!

DOL. But we'll have to make up the fire; since we opened the balcony a while ago the room has become very cold. (*Stirring the fire.*)

CAR. It's true. But let him not receive the full heat. We must place the screen in front—so. (*Places it.*)

DOL. It is well—so.

CAR. (*going to the balcony and raising the curtain*). Look—look! The sky has become a little cleared, and the moon has issued from the clouds. Very beautiful! Very beautiful! We must draw the curtain back, that Lazarus may see it all and be the more inspired. I know he likes to work while gazing towards the heavens from time to time.

DOL. (*running to help* CARMEN). You are right; you think of everything.

JAV. Well, if after so many precautions and such endearments the inspiration is not responsive, the inspiration of Lazarus is hard to please.

CAR. Is everything ready now?

Dol. I think so. Wait—your portrait is hidden in the shade. We must place it so that the lamp may throw light on it, so that he may be inspired by it also.

Car. I inspire him? Yes—yes! Take it away. (*Wishing to remove it.*)

Dol. I shall not allow it. Let it remain where I have put it, and let us go.

Car. If you insist—well, then let him see it. But there is not much light. (*Turning up the light of the lamp.*)

Dol. (*to* Javier). Call him—let him come.

Car. Yes, let him come and write something very beautiful. Then I shall enter for a moment, to bid him good-night.

Dol. Until then—come, Carmen.

Car. (*to* Javier). And you, too, leave him alone; you must not have any more privileges than we.

Dol. Are you coming to keep us company?

Jav. Later on.

Car. Is everything in order? (*Looking round.*)

Dol. I think so. Adieu.

Car. Adieu!

> [*Exeunt to left* Carmen *and* Dolores, *half embracing each other.*

Jav. The field is clear. Poor women! How they love him! It is adoration. (*Going to right.*) Lazarus! Good-for-nothing! Now you can come—come, if you can!

> *Enter* Lazarus, *pale, somewhat in disorder, and with unsteady step; in short, as the actor may think fit.*

Laz. (*looking about*). Are they not here?

Jav. No; fortunately it occurred to them that you would work better alone.

THE SON OF DON JUAN.

LAZ. Well, whatever you say, I think that I am presentable. Eh? My head doesn't feel bad—a delicious vagueness. I seem to be encircled by a mist—a very soft mist; and through its texture there shine some little stars. In short, peaceful sensations, very peaceful.

JAV. That's to say, you are better?

LAZ. Don't I tell you so? My legs indeed give way, but without pain. I walk in the midst of softness. (*Laughing.*) My head among the clouds and the ground of cotton-wool. Divine! So ought the universe to be—that is, *quilted*. Lord! what a world has been made of it—so rough, so hard, so inconvenient. At every step you stumble and injure yourself—rocks, rugged stones, sharp points, peaks, angles, and little corners and big corners. The world should be round—quite so, and round it is; roundness is perfection; but it should be an immeasurable sphere of eider-down, so that, if a citizen falls, he may always fall amid softness—thus! (*Letting himself fall in the arm-chair, or on one of the cushioned stools at the side of the table.*)

JAV. All very well—but you really are not strong.

LAZ. I am not strong? Stronger than you—stronger than you. Stronger.

JAV. I told you that you should not drink. It does you harm; your health is broken down.

LAZ. I'm broken down? I?—How? I have not been a saint, but neither have I been a madman. I am young: I have always thought that I was strong: and, through drinking two or three glasses, and smoking a puro and laughing a little—here am I transformed into a stupid being! Because, now, it is not that I am broken down, as you say, nor that I am drunk, as you suppose—it is that I feel simply stupid.

No; and see, now, it is not so disagreeable to be stupid : one feels—a sort of merriment, as it were. That's why so many people are merry. (*Laughing.*) That's why! That's why! Now I am falling into this same stupidity—that's why, just so.

JAV. Attend to me, and understand what I say to you, if you are in a condition to understand me.

LAZ. If I can understand you? I understand everything now. The world is transparent to me: your head is made of crystal (*laughing*), and written in very black and tortuous letters I read your thought—you suppose I am very bad. Poor Javier! (*Laughing.*)

JAV. Don't talk such rubbish : I neither think such a thing, nor are you really ill. Fatigue, weariness— nothing more. You have lived very fast in Madrid during the last few years : you have thought much, you have worked much, you have had a good deal of pleasure, and you need a few months' rest—here—in your father's house, with your mother, with Carmen.

LAZ. Carmen—yes—look at her. (*Pointing to the photograph.*) There she is. How sad, how poetical, how adorable a countenance. I wish to live for her. With all the glory that I achieve I shall make a circle of light for that dear, pretty little head. (*Sends a kiss to the portrait.*) We shall live together, you and I, my sweet little Carmen, and we shall be very happy. (*As if speaking with her.*) For I wish to live. (*Growing excited and turning to* JAVIER.) If I had never lived it would never have suggested itself to me that I should continue to live : but I have commenced, and I don't wish to break off so soon. No—no—it shall not be—as God lives.

JAV. Come, Lazarus.

LAZ. I am strong. Why should I not be so?

What right has nature to make of me a feeble creature when I wish to be strong? My thought burns, my heart leaps, my veins abound with the exuberance of life, my desires are aflame! To put steam of a thousand atmospheres into an old and rusty boiler! Oh! infamous mockery!

JAV. Eh! There you are, started off! What steam, or what boiler? The little glass of champagne.

LAZ. A man like myself cannot be tormented with impunity. Here you have the world: it is yours: run merrily through its valleys, mount its summits in triumph! But you shall not run, you shall not mount, unless rheumatism is planted in your bones. Here you have the azure firmament: it is yours: fly among its altitudes, gaze upon its horizons. But you shall not fly except the plumage of your wings be wrenched away and you become a worm-eaten carcass. What derision! What satire! What cruelty! Accursed wine! What extravagant things I see, Javier! Colossal figures in masks float across the firmament, and, hung from very long strings, which are suspended from very long canes, they bear suns and splendours and stars, and they sweep onward crying, "Hurrah! hurrah!"[1] and I wish to reach all that, and I cannot touch even one little star with my lips. Grotesque, very grotesque! Cruel! very cruel! Sorrowful, very sorrowful! My God! My God! (*He hides his face in his hands.*)

JAV. Come, Lazarus, come. You see you cannot commit even the slightest excess.

LAZ. I have uttered many follies, have I not? No

[1] The original "al higui! al higui!" is a term of rejoicing peculiar to children in their games. It is only used in the South of Spain.

matter: no one hears me but you, and it's a relief to me. See, now I am more composed. I feel tired, and I even think I am sleepy.

Jav. That would be best for you: sleep, sleep, and let neither your mother nor Carmen see you thus.

Laz. As for my mother, it would not matter. (*Smiling.*) But, Carmen—let not Carmen see me looking ridiculous. The poor girl who imagines that I am a superior being! Poor child, what a joke! (*Stretches himself on the sofa.*)

Jav. Good; now don't speak. I shall not speak either; and try to sleep. With half an hour of sleep everything will pass off.

Laz. Sleep, too, is ridiculous at times. If I am very ridiculous don't let Carmen see me.

Jav. No; if you don't look as beautiful as Endymion she shall not enter.

Pause. Javier *walks about.* Lazarus *begins to sleep.*

Laz. Javier, Javier.

Jav. What?

Laz. Now I am—almost asleep. How do I look?

Jav. Very poetical.

Laz. Good—thank—you. Very poetical.

A pause.

Jav. No, Lazarus is not well. I shall speak to his father—no, not to Don Juan. To his mother, who is the only person of sense in this house.

Laz. Javier.

Jav. What do you want?

Laz. Put Carmen's picture more to the front.

Jav. So?

Laz. So. For her—the light; for Lazarus—the gloom.

JAV. (*walking about slowly*). Yes, I shall speak to his mother. And—happy coincidence! I had not remembered that the celebrated Doctor Bermudez, a specialist in all that relates to the nervous system, has arrived within the last few days. Then to him! let them consult with him.

LAZ. (*now almost asleep*). Javier.

JAV. But are you not going to sleep?

LAZ. Yes—but more in the light—more in the light. (*With a somewhat sorrowful accent.*)

JAV. Come (*placing the portrait close to the light*)— and silence.

LAZ. Yes . . . Carmen ! . . .

JAV. (*contemplating him for a while.*) Thank God —asleep.

DOLORES, CARMEN, DON JUAN, *and* TIMOTEO *appear at the threshold of the door at the back centre.*

CAR. May we come in?

JAV. Silence!

CAR. It was to say good-night.

JAV. He is asleep. He worked a short time, but he was fatigued.

CAR. Then let us not disturb him. Adieu, Javier. The light is in his eyes—you should lower the shade. Adieu. (*Kissing* DOLORES.) Adieu, Don Juan.

TIM. (*to* DOL.) Till to-morrow. (*To* DON J.) Till to-morrow.

JUAN. Nor shall we let to-morrow go by. I shall pay you a solemn visit—and prepare yourself, little rogue (*to* CARMEN).

CAR. I?

JUAN. Silence, he is asleep.

TIM. Good, good. Ah! it is late. Good-bye.

Dol. Good-bye, my daughter.
All have spoken in low voices.
[*Exeunt* Carmen *and* Timoteo.
Dol. (*approaching* Javier.) Did he work long?

Jav. A short time, but with great ardour. A great effort of intellect.

Juan (*approaching also and contemplating* Lazarus). Lord, to think of what this boy is going to be! The face foretells it. The aureola of talent!

Dol. He is very pale—very pale.

Juan. What would you have him to be? Fat as a German, and red as a beetroot? Then he would not be a genius.

Dol. However—such pallor!

Juan *and* Dolores *are bent over* Lazarus *contemplating him with affectionate care.*

Juan. I am decidedly the father of a genius, and then (*to* Javier) they come to me with——

Jav. With what?

Juan. With nothing. (*Aside.*) With moral sermons, and with the law of heredity, and with all that stale trash. The father a hare-brained fellow, and the son a wise man.

Dol. But has nothing been amiss with him? Was it nothing more than fatigue?

Jav. Nothing more. You may withdraw: I shall stay until he awakes.

Juan. I shall not withdraw. I was wanting nothing better. I shall sit down here (*sitting at the other side of the table*), and from here I shall watch the sleep of Lazarus. You remain on foot, in honour of the genius. Keep away, keep away from before him, that you may not prevent me from seeing my son.

DOL. Yet the sleep is not very restful.

JUAN. How should it be restful, woman, since he must be busied with great matters in his dreams?

DOL. My Lazarus.

JAV. (*aside.*) Poor Lazarus.

JUAN (*laughing quietly*). Don Juan Tenorio—watching the sleep—of the son of Don Juan!—silence—silence—let's see if we shall hear anything from the son of Don Juan. (*With pride and tenderness.*)

END OF ACT I

ACT II.

Same appointments as in first Act. It is day. On the little table are flowers. DON JUAN *discovered seated close to the tea-table.* LAZARUS *also discovered. He sometime walks about; again he sits down: he tries to write, he throws away the pen. He opens a book and reads for a few moments, closes it irritably and resumes his walking about. It is evident that he is uneasy and nervous. All this in the course of the scene with his father.* DON JUAN *follows him with his eyes and smokes a puro.*

JUAN. What are you thinking of? Ah! pardon! I must not disturb you.

LAZ. You don't disturb me, father. I was thinking of nothing important. My imagination was wandering, and I was wandering after it.

JUAN. If you wish to work—to write—to read—and I trouble you I shall go. Ha, I shall go. (*Rising.*) Do you want me to go? for here I am going.

LAZ. No, father, good gracious! You disturb me!

JUAN (*siting down again*). The fact is, as you see, that which I do can be done anywhere. It is in substance nothing. Well, for the performance of nothing any point of space is good. (*Laughing.*) Of space! There are your philosophical offshoots taking root in me. The father in space, the son in the fifth heaven. That's why I say if I disturb——

LAZ. No, father, don't go away; and let us talk of what you please.

JUAN. Much good you'd get by talking with me. To your great books, to your papers, to those things which astound by their greatness and are admired for their beauty! Continue—continue! I shall see you at work. I, too, shall busy myself with something. (*Pulls the bell.*)

LAZ. As you like. [*Sits down and writes fitfully.*
Enter TERESA.

JUAN. Little Teresa—(*looking at his son and correcting himself.*) Teresa, bring me a glass of sherry and a few biscuits; I also have to busy myself with something. And bring me the French newspapers; no, nothing but *Figaro* and *Gil Blas*. (*To his son.*) And so we shall both be at work. (*To* TERESA.) Listen—by the way, bring me that novel which is in my room. You can read, can't you?

TER. Yes, señor.

JUAN. Well, then, a book which says *Nana*—you understand?

TER. Yes, señor. Ná-ná.—For no is ná.

JUAN. It is something, little girl,—(*aside*) something that you will be in time. [*Exit* TERESA.

LAZ. (*Rises and walks about—aside*). I have no ideas. To-day I have no ideas. Yes, I have many; but they come like a flight of birds; they flutter about —and they go.

JUAN. See now—I cannot bear immoral novels.

LAZ. You said . . . ?

JUAN. Nothing! I thought that you said something. I said that I cannot endure immoral novels. (*Assum-*

ing airs of austerity.) I read them, I read "Nana," out of curiosity, as a study, but I can't bear them. Literature is in a lost condition, my son, in a lost condition. Nemesio lent me that book—and I am anxious to have done with it.

LAZ. Zola is a great writer. (*Aside.*) This is the very thing that I was looking for. (*He sits and writes.*)

 Enter TERESA *with a tray, a bottle of sherry, a glass and the biscuits, "*Nana*" and the two newspapers.*

TER. Here is everything. The sherry: the newspapers just come, the tender little biscuits, and the tender little *Nana* (baby) as well. (*She stands looking at the two gentlemen.*)

JUAN. Bring the sherry closer, Teresa.—Work, boy, work. Take no notice of me. Work, for it is thus that men attain success. I also in my youth have worked much. That's the reason I look so old. (*Staring at* TERESA *who laughs.*) (*Aside.*) What's that stupid girl laughing at?—(*To* TERESA.) Now, you may go. I don't want you. The *Gil Blas!* (*Unfolds it and begins to read it.*) Let us have a look at these wretched little newspapers.... (*affecting contempt.*) I told you to go.—(*To* TERESA.)—Let's see, let's see. (*Reads.*)

TER. Yes, señor. (*She remains for a while looking at the two, and turns towards the door in the back centre.*)

LAZ. (*rising*). Teresa—

TER. Señorito—

LAZ. Come here and speak lower: let us not disturb your master, who is reading. Did you take the letter which I gave you this morning?

TER. Yes, señorito, I took it myself. Whatever you require me to do, señorito! . . . . . .

Laz. Good. It was for Señor Bermudez, eh?

Ter. Yes, señorito. That doctor who has such a great name, who has come from Madrid for a few days to cure Don Luciano Barranco—the same who, they say, is either mad or not mad. (*Laughing.*)

Laz. (*starting, then restraining himself*). Ah! Yes. Quite so; the same. And did you see him? Did you hand him the letter? Did he give you the answer? Where is it? Come, quick!

Ter. Eh, señorito—

Laz. Come—

Ter. I gave the letter: he was not in :—they said—

Laz. Lower—(*Looking at his father who laughs while reading the newspaper.*)

Ter. They said that as soon as he came back they would give him the letter. Have no fear, señorito. Whatever little I take charge of! Well, if I do nothing worse than—

Laz. It's well—thanks. (*Dismissing her, then recalling her.*) Oh! if they bring the answer—here on the instant—eh?

Ter. On the instant : I should think so ! have no fear, señorito.

Laz. Enough! let us not trouble my father.

[*Exit* Teresa.

Juan. Ha! ha! ha! Facetious, very facetious! sprightly, very sprightly! Pungent as a capsicum from the Rioja! It is the only newspaper that one can read!

Laz. Some interesting article? What is it? What does it say? Let me see! (*Approaching and stretching out his hand.*)

Juan (*keeping back the newspaper*). A very shameless little article—and quite without point. It must be put away. (*Puts it in a pocket of his dressing-gown, but in such a way that it may be seen.*) May the devil not so contrive things that Carmen may come and find the newspaper and read it in all innocence.

LAZ. (*withdrawing*). It is true: you do well! *Walks about nervously.*)

JUAN (*aside*). And I had not finished reading it: I shall read it afterwards. (*Takes up* "Nana.") This also is good. The spring with all its verdure. (*Aloud.*) Work, boy, work!

LAZ. (*aside*). I shall speak to the Doctor this very day, that he may set my mind at ease. I know that nothing is the matter with me; but I want a specialist to assure me on the point. And then, with mind at peace—to my drama, to my critico-historical work, to my æsthetic theories which are new, completely new—and to Carmen. And with the muse at one side, recounting marvels in my ear, and with Carmen on the other side, pressed against my heart—to enjoy life, to inhale the odour of triumphs, to live for love, to satiate my longings amidst eternal mysteries.

JUAN. Stupendous! Monumental! Sufficient to make one die of laughing. Lord, why does a man read? To be amused; then books that are amusing for me! (*Laughing.*)

LAZ. Is that a nice book?

JUAN (*changing his tone*). Pshaw—yes—pretty well. But these frivolous things are tiresome after all. (*Sees* LAZARUS *coming towards him, and puts* "Nana" *into the other pocket of the dressing-gown.*) Have you anything solid to read—really substantial?

LAZ. I have many large books. What class do you want?

JUAN. Something serious; something that instructs you, that makes you think.

LAZ. (*going to the bookcase*). Would you like something of Kant?

JUAN. Of Kant? Do you say of Kant? Quite so! he was my favourite author. When I was young I went to sleep every night reading Kant. (*Aside.*) What will that be? It sounds like a dog.

LAZ. (*searching out a passage*). If you like, I shall tell you.

JUAN. No, my lad; any part whatever! (*Taking the book.*) Yes, this may be read at any part. You shall see. And don't concern yourself with me; write, my son, write.

LAZARUS *sits and attempts to write.* DON JUAN *reads.*

"Under the aspect of relationship, the third consequence of taste, the beautiful appears to us as the final form of an object, without representation of end." The devil! (*holding the book far off, as long-sighted people do and contemplating it with terror.*) The devil! "or as a finality without end." Whoever can understand this? "Because what is called final form is the causality of any conception whatever with relation to the object." Let me see—let me see. (*Holding the book still further off.*) "Final form the causality." I believe I am perspiring. (*Wipes his forehead.*) "The consciousness of this finality without end is the play of the cognitive forces." How does he say that? "The play of the forces—the play." Well, I ought to understand this about play. "The consciousness of this internal causality is that which constitutes the æsthetic pleasure." If I go on it will give me a congestion. Jesus, Mary and Joseph!

And to think that Lazarus understands about the finality without end, the causality and the play of the cognitive forces! God help me! What a boy!—(*continues reading.*) "The principle of the formal convenience of nature is the transcendental principle of the force of Judgment." (*Giving a blow on the table.*) I shall be lost if I continue reading. But if that boy reads these things he will go mad.

Laz. Does it interest you?

Juan. Very much! What depth! (*Aside.*) For five minutes I have been falling, and I have not reached the bottom. (*Aloud.*) I should think it does interest me! But, frankly, I prefer—

Laz. Hegel?

Juan. Exactly. (*Aside*)—"Nana." But you, my son, neither read, nor write: you are fretful. What's the matter with you? Did the hunting tire you? Yet the exercise of the chase is very healthy for one who like you wears himself away over his books. Are you ill?

Laz. No, señor, I am not ill. And I spent these three days in the country very pleasantly. But this morning broke dull and rainy, and I said—"Home!"

Juan. And you arrived when I was getting up. I told you the great news; immediately you showed great delight; but then you fell into sublime preoccupations. Poor Carmen! (*approaching him with an air of secrecy.*) You don't love her as she loves you.

Laz. With all my soul! More than you can imagine! I am as I am: reserved, untamed, unpolished—but I know how to love!

Juan. Better and better! The poor little thing—come, now—the poor little thing.

Laz. And why did not Don Timoteo answer on

the spot that he accepted? When you asked him for his daughter for me, why did he hesitate?

JUAN. What do you mean by hesitation? I do him the honour of requesting the hand of Carmen for my Lazarus—and he would hesitate! I should strangle the scarecrow. Marry a man like you! What more could any daughter or any father desire?

LAZ. Then why did he put off the answer till to-day?

JUAN. The prescriptions of etiquette: social conventionalities: he was always a great stickler for etiquette. Because he must consult with Carmen. Imagine him consulting with Carmen! When the poor little thing is like a soul in purgatory, and you are her heaven.—Ha! ha!

LAZ. You are right.

JUAN. No: you shall have your sweet little wife, your home; you shall work hard, you shall gain great glory, you shall keep a sound judgment—and let the whole world say: Don Lazarus Mejia, son of Don Juan Mejia! Oh!

LAZ. Yes, señor: I shall do what I can—and I shall love my Carmen dearly.

JUAN. That's right—that's right. But something's the matter with you. You seem as it were absent-minded.

LAZ. I am thinking—of my drama.

JUAN. Then I shall go! decidedly I shall go! With my insipid chatter I prevent you from thinking. Oh! thought! the—the—(*looking at the book*) " the cognitive forces "—the—the—(*looking again*) " the finality "—that's it—" the finality."—Ah!—Good-bye.

LAZ. But don't go away on my account.

JUAN. We must show respect to the wise. (*Laughing.*) I am going to read all alone the great book which you have lent me. (*Taking a flower and putting it in the buttonhole of his dressing-gown.*) Consider now, whether I shall hesitate between Kant and "Nana." (*Pulls the bell.*)

LAZ. As you please.

JUAN. Good-bye, my son. To your drama—to your drama—and put nothing immoral in it.

Enter TERESA.

TER. Señor.—

JUAN. Listen, Teresa: take all that to my room. Wait—(*Pours himself out a glass. Touching one pocket.*) Here is *Gil Blas*, (*touching*) here is "Nana": Kant hauled along by the neck—and to my room. Work, my boy, work! Do something great. Leave something to the world. I shall leave you—I think—(*drinking the glass of wine.*) Well, this finality—has an end. To work—to work?—Good-bye. Lord, what a Lazarus this is! To my room with all that, little Teresa.

[*Exit carrying in one pocket* Gil Blas, *in the other* "Nana," *in his buttonhole the flower, and gripped very hard the volume of Kant.*

LAZ. Teresa, they have brought no letter for me?

TER. (*preparing to remove the wine and the biscuits*). No, señor.

LAZ. Patience: you did not tell my mother I had written to that Señor de Bermudez.

TER. No, señor.

LAZ. Has my mother got up?

TER. Got up, indeed! Before you returned this morning from hunting, Doña Dolores had already gone to call for the Señorita Carmen that they might go to Mass together.

LAZ. Good.

TER. And I don't know how she rose so early, nor how she found courage to go out.

LAZ. Why?

TER. Because last night she was very ill : very ill indeed.

LAZ. (*starting up*). My mother!

TER. Yes, señor. I say that it must have been the nerves. How she cried: how she twisted her arms! Indeed I wanted to send an express messenger for you to come back at once.

LAZ. Ah! my God, my poor mother! and why was I not informed? I would have mounted on horseback; and in one hour—here.

TER. Because the señora would not have it so. "Silence, not a word to anybody," so she said, and an order from her is an order.

LAZ. But how is it possible? My father said nothing to me!

TER. He was not informed: he went to the theatre, afterwards to the Casino with Don Timoteo and Don Nemesio; he returned late, and as the señora had given orders—"to nobody"—nothing was said to him; and he knew nothing.

LAZ. But how was it? Why was it? She who is never ill!

TER. I don't know. The señora dined early and alone. Afterwards she went out. She came back at ten o'clock: she could scarcely enter her room, and immediately fell to the ground—just like a tower that falls.

LAZ. My God! my God! And you never informed me!

TER. Well, I am informing you now. And in spite of what she said, "not a word." But as to you—for your sake! Oh! when it concerns you, señorito. (LAZARUS *pays no attention to her.*) But don't be distressed: this morning already she was so strong and so well: yes, really, very pale and with such dark circles round the eyes! but so strong. We women are thus: now we are dying and afterwards we revive: we go back to death and again we return to life.

LAZ. You mean that now she is well? But entirely well?

TER. Don't I tell you she is as well as could be? Let your mind rest, señorito.

LAZARUS, *very much agitated, has been walking about.*

LAZ. Good, good, if it has already passed off—in short, when my mother returns, tell me.

TER. You have no other orders?

LAZ. No. (*A bell rings several times.*) My father is calling: go, go quickly. The vibrating of the bell makes me nervous.

TER. I must take away this. (*Takes up the trays.*)

LAZ. (*the bell continues ringing*). Take it away quickly for pity's sake.

TER. On the instant; what a hurry that good gentleman is in!

LAZ. And if they bring the answer from Señor de Bermudez.

TER. Immediately afterwards. (*The bell continues.*) I am coming, I am coming. (*She says this without calling aloud, as if to herself.*)

[*Exit* TERESA.

LAZ. (*alone*). What she has told me about my poor mother has unstrung all my nerves. I am not well. Bah! I am not ill. How Doctor Bermudez will laugh at me when I consult him. The fact is that I am very apprehensive; but I feel strong: Javier says to me every moment : " My boy, don't strut about on your heels so much." Steady ; so, steady. (*He walks about, treads with his heels and laughs.*) I know now what's the matter. I am very happy and I have a horrible dread of losing so much happiness. Very happy. (*Counting on his fingers.*) My father and mother, so good ; Carmen, who adores me ; I, who am raving about her ; glory, which calls me ; I who answer, " Forward, Lazarus " ; my eyes, which are my own and are never satiated with drinking in light and colours ; my thought, which is mine, and which does not tire of originating wonders ; my life, which is mine, and which desires to live more, to live more—yes, more ! (*A pause.*) They say that life is dull, that it is mournful. Buffoons ! Has anything better been discovered ? Is it better to be stone which has no nerves to quiver with delight ? Is it better to be water which always runs in headlong stupidity without knowing where it goes ? Is it better to be air to blow without motive and to fill itself with the foulest earth and dust? No, it is better to be Lazarus. (*Resumes the counting on his fingers.*) For Lazarus has very good parents ; he has Carmen ; he has glory ; he has life ; and he has, above all, thought, reason ! Ha ! I have all this : I have it : what remains to be done if I have it ! (*Sits down in a somewhat cowering manner.*) It is evident—because all this is so good, and because I have it, I am afraid to lose it. I am as terrified as a little child ; at times it seems to me that I am a little child, and I am seized with impulses to run to my mother and wrap myself round in her skirt. A man who almost understands Kant and Hegel ; who writes dramas which are very well received, yes, señor, very well received ; who meditates transcendental works. A man, in every sense a man, who has fought duels in Madrid, and has had a little love affair or so—(*laughing*)—and very pleasant too: the practical reason, not of Kant but of Zola, which turns the Pure Reason of Kant into ridicule and makes even the good matron laugh. Well then, this formidable Lazarus at times is a child, and he would like his mother to embrace him and to buy him toys! To be a child, yes; all the same it is good to be a child. Nay. I should like it. (*Laughing.*) But what absurdities! Lord, what absurdities! (*Remains cowering in his chair, thinking and laughing very low.*)

Enter TERESA.

TER. Señorito, a gentleman has given me this card.

LAZ. (*as if awaking*). A gentleman? Let me see —Doctor Bermudez! But why has he put himself to inconvenience? I would have gone to him. Let him come in. Let him come in. Quick, woman, let him come in. (*Exit* TERESA.) With this man I must have much prudence, much composure, much calm. If he had heard the nonsense that I was talking! What a terror!

TERESA. (*re-entering and announcing*). Señor de Bermudez. [*Exit* TERESA.

Enter BERMUDEZ.

BERM. Señor Don Lazarus Mejia?

LAZ. Your servant—very much your servant—one who is grieved to the heart for having troubled a person such as you. A man of eminence—a man of knowledge. (*With much courtesy, but endeavouring to restrain himself.*)

BERM. Not so—not so—I received your letter.

LAZ. Indeed, it was not meant that you should give yourself any trouble. I begged you to be good enough to appoint a time for me and I should have gone to your house. But take a seat. I cannot allow you to remain standing an instant longer. Sit down! (*Making him sit down.*) Here—no—here—you will be better here.

BERM. Many thanks. You are very amiable! (*Takes a seat.*)

LAZ. I don't know whether I am entitled to sit down in the presence of a man like yourself; a national glory! (*Commands himself so that his accent is natural: perhaps however he errs a little by excess of courtesy.*)

BERM. For goodness' sake!

LAZ. A man of European fame!

BERM. You overwhelm me. I don't deserve— (*Aside.*) He is very engaging, this young man. They were right in Madrid to say that he has plenty of ability.

LAZ. You don't deserve it? Ah! in the mouth of a celebrity like Doctor Bermudez, modesty will always have a voice, but it has no vote.

BERM. Señor de Mejia. (*Aside.*) How well he speaks!

LAZ. Don't treat me ceremoniously. I am not deserving of so much solemnity. "Señor de Mejia"! (*Laughing.*) Call me Lazarus. I really don't deserve anything better; treat me as a master might a pupil. I dare not say as a kind friend would treat a respectful friend.

BERM. As you please. It will be an honour for me! (*Aside.*) Very engaging, very engaging!

LAZ. Well, I repeat that I am sorry at heart for having given you this trouble.

BERM. Not at all. I already told your mother last night that if at any other time she required me, or if she wished by any further suggestions to make me amplify my opinion, I was unconditionally at her orders. A card saying to me " Come," and I should come instantly. And so it is that on receiving the letter this morning—as you may imagine—I said, " I must place myself at the feet of that lady, and I must personally become acquainted with her son, a national glory of the future, one who is destined to have a European renown."

Laz. Señor de Bermudez! (*Repudiating the honour with a gesture. Aside.*) My mother—last night—what does he say? (*Commanding himself, then aloud.*) So my mother went last night—to see you—because——

Berm. Yes, señor, she has already explained everything to me. That you were out hunting, and that you did not mean to return this week; that she had been informed that I was going back to Madrid this day, and that she had been anxious to consult me without the loss of a moment concerning the illness of that poor young man—a cousin or a nephew, or a relative—I think he is a nephew of your mother, whose name she said was — Don Luis — Don Luis——

Laz. Quite so—*a nephew.* You have it. (*Smiling. Then aside.*) What's this? What relative is that? Why, it is not true. God of Heaven! (*Aloud.*) A nephew—that's it. To whom God does not give sons, the devil,—— (*Laughing.*) Yes, but she also has me —her Lazarus, her son!

Berm. And she must be proud.

Laz. Señor de Bermudez, have compassion on a beginner. But I wish you to explain to me what you had the kindness to explain to my mother; because ladies—don't understand much about medical science

—and though I understand just as little of it, nevertheless——

BERM. Quite so ; it is a speciality.

LAZ. A speciality, that's it ; it is a speciality. And moreover, I know that young man more intimately—poor Luis ! And I can supply you with fresh particulars.

BERM. Oh ! those of your mother were very precise. She has a keenly observant mind.

LAZ. Very much so ; don't you describe it well ! A keenly observant mind. (*Aside*.) My God !—my mother—and on her return home—her weeping—what does this man say ?

BERM. Altogether it would be better that I should see the poor young man ; but should that not be possible——

LAZ. I should think it is possible, and that would be the best. You shall see him. I myself will take him to you—to your house. Yes, señor, to your house ; yes, señor.

BERM. That will do perfectly. That was what I said to your mother, but she told me in reply that so long as things don't come to an extremity, families require to consider. I understand and I impute no blame.

LAZ. Nothing of the kind. Now, at this very moment you shall come with me to see that—that poor young man. A man like you ! Why, there's no difficulty about it.

BERM. (*rising*). Then I await your orders.

LAZ. Allow me, my friend, my dear friend : first of all I should like—I beg of you to tell me what my mother explained to you, and what was your opinion ; because, although she related everything to me this morning, I should be glad to hear it from your lips.

One learns everything by listening to such a man as Doctor Bermudez. (*In a persuasive tone.*) I am so anxious that you should speak, and that I should hear you. Indeed, it has been the dream of my existence. Speak, speak.

BERM. Dear Lazarus. (*Aside.*) I have fascinated him, decidedly. (*Aloud.*) Your mother explained to me with great lucidity all the antecedents of the patient: his sufferings when a child, his character, his studies, his excitable imagination, the first symptoms of the illness, a fainting attack, another more violent.

LAZ. (*somewhat drily*). All that I know already. Go on. (*With extreme cordiality.*) Go on, my dear Bermudez.

BERM. The doctor is rather like a confessor, and your mother did not object to letting me know of the youthful days of the father—of the father of the young man.

LAZ. Ah! his youthful days—yes—his youthful days—yes—yes—and what else?

BERM. His vicious conduct; his unbridled libertinism——

LAZ. (*excitedly*). Libertinism! (*Controlling himself.*) Yes. (*With a forced laugh.*) Follies of youth. A lady always exaggerates these things. I have not been a saint myself; neither have you. Doctor, doctor, you with all your science and all your gravity. God knows. God knows! Oh! these doctors! (*Giving him a slap on the back.*) And what more?

BERM. (*laughing*). We are mortals and sinners, friend Lazarus.

LAZ. And we take for fine gold little lenses of talc. Come, come to the talc.

BERM. Thus stands the case—that that good

gentleman, the father of the patient, reached the age of gravity, and he was not a steady man, and he did not correct his faults. His wife seems to have suffered very much. Is all this exact which your mother told me? Because if it is exact it must be taken into account. That's the reason I ask.

LAZ. (*aside*). My head! Oh my head! (*Succeeds in commanding himself, and speaks naturally. Aloud.*) See, doctor, those are details of which I know nothing. But if my mother told you so, it will be true. My mother is a superior spirit, a most pure soul, a mother beyond comparison. But let us not speak of the mother, only of the son, that's to say of the son of the other mother. Therefore let's see, let's see. What more did she tell you?

BERM. That to prevent the son from becoming fully acquainted with the disorders of the father— because the boy, naturally, was growing up, the mother had to send him to a college in France.

LAZ. (*aside*). It is I. It is I! Ah! ah! Calm! let me be calm!

BERM. What do you say?

LAZ. Nothing. I laugh at those family tragedies— the father a madcap, and the son,—— And as you fill me with such respect—and as the subject is so sad —I should not have presumed to laugh. Ah! Señor de Bermudez, what a world this is!—what a world this is! Come, come. (*Growing calm.*) Yes, señor, the history, so far as I know, is entirely correct. Then they sent him to study in Madrid—that unfortunate, unfortunate youth: but, look you, not so unfortunate—for he went through his course with distinction.

BERM. Quite so, and the father remained always the same.

Laz. (*somewhat harshly*). Let us not speak of the father. And why? Because the son is now launched on the world; then let us leave out of the question the other. (*Recollecting himself.*) Ah! pardon me. I love my father so much, I respect him so much, that those words which you uttered have caused me much pain, much pain. A weakness I confess; a man of science does not know those weaknesses; but we poets are thus. You—you raise yourselves above the level of human miseries. The eagle soars alike—eh? above the peak of granite with its robe of frost—eh? and over the infected puddle—or the mire—the mire —eh? But we are not all as Doctor Bermudez? (*Grasping his hand.*)

Berm. I respect your delicacy: but science is implacable. A father who has consumed his life in vice—

LAZARUS *retreats in his chair.*

Who has wallowed with all the energies of his nature in the mire of riot, who has heated his blood in the embers of all impure fires—runs the danger of transmitting to his son nothing but the germs of death or the germs of madness!

LAZARUS *recoils more and more.*

And I tell you, as I told your mother last night, without prejudice to the rectification of my opinion when I have examined the patient, that if the description which you have given me is exact—and I conclude that it is——

Laz. It is. What then?

Berm. Ah! the springs of life cannot be corrupted with impunity. *The Son of that father* will very soon sink into madness or into idiocy. A madman or an idiot: such is his fate!

(*He says this without looking round, with solemnity, like one who pronounces a sentence: gazing forward and motioning with his arm towards* LAZARUS. *The latter cowers in his chair and looks at* BERMUDEZ *with horror.*)

LAZ. Ah! No! What? My father! I! A lie! A lie! It is a lie! (*Hides his face in his hands.*)

BERM. What's this? Lazarus! Señor de Mejia! Are you ill? What do you say? (*Rising and approaching* LAZARUS.) I don't understand! Can it be? What?

LAZ. That I am the madman? Silence! That I am the idiot? Silence! That I am such—I? Look at me well: study me well: strengthen your judgment: meditate, examine, give sentence!

BERMUDEZ *standing,* LAZARUS *seated and clutching the doctor by the arm.*

BERM. But this is not fair, Señor de Mejia! This is not just! By God—by the Holy God!

LAZ. Fairness, justice, in a man such as I? Bermudez, Bermudez, I did wrong, I confess—(*with a mixture of courtesy, sadness, and some sarcasm*)—An idiot who presents his most humble excuses to a wise man! Be generous, pardon me.

BERM. You have not understood me. I am sorry for you, Lazarus, because I have given you—a shock —a bad time of it, without cause—believe me, without any cause. God help me, these dramatic authors—no, one is not safe with them! (*Wishing to turn the matter off with a laugh.*)

LAZ. Let us be calm, let us be calm. I want the truth; there still remains to me some glimmer of reason, and I can understand what you say to me. Ha! the truth—Bermudez, the truth! It is the last truth that

I can understand, and I wish to enjoy it. (*Rising.*) Out with it! I still understand—yes—still!

BERM. Friend Lazarus! By all the saints of the heavenly court!——

LAZ. No, I still keep my senses; I shall explain to you all that has passed. My mother, pretending to inquire about another, inquired about me; I, pretending to be interested on another's account, was interested on my own, and a poor mother and a lost wretch have between them cajoled a wise man. Ah! cajoled—no: pardon. We wished to know the truth—nothing more; but as the truth is treacherous, it is necessary at times to drag it forth by treason. I humbly beg that you will pardon us—my mother—and myself.

BERM. I tell you that I cannot recover from my surprise; that I am cut to the heart for having spoken with such levity. I have already told you that my opinion was haphazard—quite haphazard—without examination of the patient. (*Seeking where to go.*)

LAZ. Well, here is the patient. Don't I tell you that I am the man? Oh, have no fear: I am a man capable of looking face to face upon death, and of answering the grimace of madness with another grimace even more grotesque. While a heart remains to me, the head will obey.

BERM. For God's sake, calm yourself. All this is not serious.

LAZ. I am perfectly calm; I am still master of myself. Sit down. (*Makes him take a seat.*) Let us talk quietly. Tell me all, but in a low voice, that my mother may not know; that she may not know. And of my father, not a word! Of my father—no, enough—nothing! I have been a madman in Madrid, so that the madness is mine. It is all mine! Oh! you deny that it is all mine? That is not right, Señor de Bermudez. Take to yourself the accusation that it is not right. You deny me my own reason, and you even wish to deprive me of my own madness, saying—saying—that my father—silence! Well, my reason may not belong to me: patience! But my madness belongs to me; I swear to you that it belongs to me, and I shall defend it—I shall defend it, Bermudez! (*Advances upon the physician. Then restrains himself.*) And now, let us talk soberly of myself—of my suffering.

BERM. Señor de Mejia, dear Lazarus—as for what I told you a while since, it was purely hypothetical; now that I know you, I modify my opinion in every point.

LAZ. (*with a mocking smile*). Indeed? By God, Señor de Bermudez, that I am a madman we'll let pass; but I am not yet an idiot.

BERM. By God, Señor de Mejia, I am sure that I shall go out of this house either an idiot or a madman!

LAZ. When do you calculate that I shall suffer the decisive attack—the last: that of eternal night; that which surrounds us with blackness for ever? How easily it is known that I have been a poet, eh? Eternal night, eternal blackness! Is it not true? However, say—when? What term do you allow me? A year? three months? or is it immediately? Candidly. You see, now, that I still hear, and understand, and even speak poetically. Eternal blackness, eternal night! However, let me know—let me know. A year, eh?

BERM. It is readily perceived that you are a poet. You plunge into the regions of phantasy. You see, your nervous system is shaken, somewhat shaken. I don't deny it; but I make myself responsible for your cure; do you want more?

LAZ. We are coming to the point. As for my cure, I am ready to believe that. But the decisive attack—when? I have such a feeling these few days past, that I think it will be very soon.

BERM. Ravings, ravings! these are ravings.

LAZ. Precisely. Ah! you have said it—ravings. Come, an effort. Will it be to-morrow, will it be to-day?

BERM. Neither to-day, nor to-morrow, nor within twenty years, if you keep your senses.

LAZ. If I keep my senses! You are ingenious. "I shall not lose my senses if I keep my senses." Naturally.

BERM. A good sign: now we are joking.

LAZ. Yes, I am very quiet. At first I felt a wave of blood roll through my brain; then a wave of ice, which spread through all my being. And now—well—quiet—tired, a little tired, nothing more.

BERM. Good; then take a rest, put your mind at ease; and before my setting out for Madrid I shall return. I have to convince you——

LAZ. I am convinced! Oh, my God! I don't wish to keep you any longer, I have sufficiently abused your kindness.

BERM. (*making a movement to withdraw*). Then if you will permit me——

LAZ. Yes, señor, assuredly (*accompanying him*). And don't have any ill-will towards me.

BERM. Good God—no; however, my friend——

LAZ. (*detaining him*). One moment! (*In his ear.*) When?

BERM. Some other time.

LAZ. No; the one thing that I wish you to tell me,

is this: "Lazarus, there is no hope; the attack will be next month, or next week, or to-morrow, or to-night, or this very hour," in short, when must it be? This is the only thing you have to tell me: I ask no more.

BERM. But how can you have me knowingly utter nonsense?

LAZ. (*energetically*). Because you have the inevitable power of telling me the truth; however sharp, however bitter, however mournful, it may be, you must tell it to me. It is a question of honour, of life or death. Now you shall understand me. (*In a low voice in the doctor's ear.*) I love, I adore Carmen; our wedding has been arranged: it will take place in a short time—within fifteen days. And now, answer me: Can I, in conscience, without being guilty of infamy, can I bind the existence of Carmen to my existence—to the existence of an idiot?

BERM. What a question!

LAZ. If you are a man of honour——. What, go away without answering me? Well, the way is free to you (*withdrawing from him*). Oh! I'll not detain you.

BERM. By God, Lazarus——

LAZ. But reflect, that through the cowardice of a moment, through not having spoken to me as one man speaks to another man—for I still am a man—you are about to do great mischief. Because if you don't say to me, "Renounce," I shall not renounce Carmen; I shall embrace her and drag her down with me to the abyss.

BERM. You see that I can do no more.

LAZ. You see that love is life—the oil of life which propagates itself. And what will be our posterity? Come, say it, boldly. A swarm of neurotics, of idiots, of lunatics, perhaps of criminals. A common sewer hurrying on to death the wrecks of humanity. In candour, in honesty, say it.

BERM. Oh! what a head! Indeed, if you continue thus, I assure you that you will go mad.

LAZ. By the memory of your mother, by the honour of your family, by the happiness of your children, by the sacred duty of your profession, by your conscience as an upright man, by your God, by piety, by compassion——, if you had a daughter would you allow her to marry me?

BERM. To-day? No! (*Wishes to continue.*)

LAZ. Enough! nor to-morrow either. Enough—never—thank you. My sentence! Carmen, Carmen! (*Falls on the sofa.*)

BERM. Lazarus—for God's sake—you did not allow me to finish. Lazarus! What a creature! Listen to me. I must call. (*Pulls the bell.*) He is losing his wits—Lazarus! (*The bell.*) Eh! Here! (*going to the door.*)

Enter DOLORES *and* DON JUAN.

BERM. Señora!

DOL. (*running to him*). Bermudez!

JUAN (*to* BERMUDEZ). My Lazarus!

DOL. (*to* BERMUDEZ). My boy!

JUAN. But what is this? Lord, what is this?

LAZ. (*rising*). Nothing. We called—they did not appear. We continued to call—and you have come. And I called because I wished to introduce you to my kind friend, Doctor Bermudez. My mother (*introducing her*); you already know each other. Is it not true that you know each other?

DOL. My son!

She and LAZARUS *embrace.*

LAZ. (*to* BERMUDEZ). Don't be surprised. As I was hunting a whole week—and as we did not see each other on my return—we were embracing.

BERM. It's natural.

LAZ. My father (*introducing him*). I have already seen my father this morning, that's why I don't embrace him. (JUAN *looks at him imploringly.*) However, that you may not imagine I love him less than my mother, I shall embrace him likewise. Father!

JUAN. Lazarus! (*Embracing him.*) Closer to me! closer! so! (*To* DOLORES, *aside.*) You see, Dolores, you see? He has such strength; he has nearly squeezed the breath out of me. It's all folly what you have been telling me.

DOL. Yes—quite true—folly.

JUAN (*to* BERMUDEZ). What's this boy suffering from?

BERM. Nothing: in substance, nothing.

JUAN (*to* DOL.). Are you listening? What a head you have!

LAZ. Make your minds easy. Delicate—slightly delicate. Don't be cast down, mother.

DOL. (*caressing him*). Lazarus, my son, my Lazarus!

JUAN (*approaching* LAZARUS *with envy*). And must I be cast down or not? Oh, it matters little whether or not I be cast down.

LAZ. Neither must you be down-hearted, father. There is no cause. I am perfectly well; let Bermudez tell you. And I am going to work for a while (*with anguish*), because I can do no more (*restraining himself*)—I can do no more with this idleness, eh? And with the regimen that you have prescribed for me

—and by following your advice—within a short time you shall see—the resurrection of Lazarus! Good-bye, Bermudez; my own mother, father and señor—illustrious doctor—note that phrase—that phrase—the resurrection of Lazarus. Ah! for this Lazarus there is no resurrection. [*Exit.*

JUAN (*to* BERMUDEZ). Speak, by Christ crucified! I know that it is nothing—but I wish you to speak. Come, my Lazarus—what? Why does this woman say such things? Jesus, Jesus, what a woman! You have always been the same. (*To* BERMUDEZ.) Don't speak lightly—these are very important matters. However, come! let me know, let me know!

BERM. Señor Don Juan, you understand—

DOL. Have you changed your opinion?

BERM. Substantially it remains unchanged.

DOL. My God! my God! (*Throws herself sobbing on a chair.*)

BERM. But we must have a little calmness; Señora, for God's sake.

JUAN. Calm? I should think so; since what you two say is impossible: then nothing else was required. As if this could do no more than come down upon a genius like Lazarus—and all in a moment. If it were I—good, because I—Señor de Bermudez—I may be puffed off any day; but Lazarus, Lazarus, consider well what you say, for these things are very important. And they must be thought over deliberately. Very important—very important indeed.

BERM. You are right, Don Juan. And now, you'll both excuse me, I am deeply affected—and I could not co-ordinate two ideas.

JUAN (*aside, to his wife*). Are you listening? He could not co-ordinate two ideas. I say, I say, why did I trust to him!

BERM. Later on—to-morrow—some other day—I shall have the pleasure of paying my compliments to you and of seeing Lazarus. Now, permit me to retire.

DOL. (*rising and hurrying towards him*). But you are not yet going back to Madrid? No, for God's sake!

BERM. No, señora. I shall remain here fifteen or twenty days longer.

DOL. Then, come again; come again, I implore you!

JUAN. Yes; come again.

BERM. Yes, señor, I shall come again.

DOL. To-morrow?

JUAN. If you gave a little look in to-night—eh? You could take coffee with us. I have some sherry——

BERM. To-night I cannot. I shall come to-morrow.

DOL. To-morrow, then, Bermudez. (*Accompanying him.*) Save my son!

JUAN. See you to-morrow, Señor de Bermudez. And have a care what you do with my Lazarus!

BERM. Till to-morrow, then, Señora. (*Pressing her hand.*) And my dear señor.

DOLORES *falls on a chair:* JUAN *walks about with difficulty, but with an air of great vigour.*

JUAN. This man does not know what he's talking about. You have now heard him; he can't co-ordinate two ideas. How simple we are! What, and do people lose their talents and lose their heads as one might lose a hat? Here, I got rid of my hat, and thus got rid of my head? Bah, bah! Idiots are what they are from infancy. Nor do I say idiots only —fools have been fools all through life; there is nobody more consistent than a fool. But as to a man of genius! Oh! Genius! Tut, absurdities of doctors!

He to pronounce judgment on my Lazarus! He who can't co-ordinate two ideas—on Lazarus, who is as familiar with the "finality without end" as he is with the *Our Father!* Come, answer. Am I right?

DOL. Would to God it might be so!

JUAN. But don't you think it is false—all that that buffoon has told us?

DOL. (*with desperation*). And if it were true? If it were true? What then? Then, why was I born? (*Advancing upon* DON JUAN, *who retreats*.) My illusions lost through you! My youth blighted through you! My dignity sneered at through you! After twenty years of sacrifices in order to be deserving of my Lazarus—good for him! loyal for him! honourable for him! And to-day? No. You have always been a wretch: but this time you are right. Impossible! Impossible! God could not let it be so.

JUAN. Well, I have been a wretch—there's no getting over it. But do not call to mind all that—and above all, don't speak of it. Say that you forgive me—forgive me, Dolores.

DOL. What does it matter to you—my forgiveness?

JUAN. It matters to us both. If you don't pardon me, and at the same time God purposes to chastise me, and chastises me in my Lazarus—" He might have been a genius, here you have in him an idiot." These things are very serious. Come come, don't say that.

DOL. What things you do say! You, too, talk at random. No matter—under such circumstances. I pardon you with all my heart.

JUAN. Thank you, Dolores. Thus we are more secure.

Dol. (*clinging to him*). But help me to save Lazarus.

Juan. With my whole soul. Though I had to give up for him all the life that remains to me.

Dol. Give your life! Ha! what life have you? All the life that God first granted you, you should give him.

Juan. Dolores!

Dol. Ah! it's true. I had pardoned you. I shall not recall my word. But what are we to do?

Juan. Take him to Madrid, that the best known physicians may see him.

Dol. Well thought of!

Juan. And then to Paris. We shall consult all the eminent men.

Dol. Quite so. Then to Germany.

Juan. And to England. The English know a great deal. Bah! there is plenty of science dispersed throughout the world.

Dol. Then we shall collect it all for Lazarus.

Juan. Without fail! All for him! Whatever remains of my fortune for him! I have squandered much, but I am still rich.

Dol. I have never called you to a reckoning. You have squandered your own.

Juan. No, señora: no, señora. It was not mine. I see it now. It belonged to Lazarus. But Lord! I did not know I was going to have Lazarus. Dolores, we must save him.

Dol. We hang on to his reason like two creatures in despair, that it may not fly away. Is it not true? (*Clinging to him.*)

Juan. Like two of the desperate, and like two parents. Is it not so? (*Pressing her to him.*) And we shall save him, eh? Don't say no; don't say no! (*Falls weeping on a sofa.*) I have been bad, but without bad intention. I did not know this. Would that I had been told! Lazarus, my Lazarus!

DOL. Don't be distressed. Don't you see that you will not have energy to struggle?

JUAN. I'll not have energy? Ah! you'll see. Ho! ho! I have no energy!

DOL. I love to see you thus. And believe me that Bermudez exaggerates.

JUAN. He is a fanatic—a buffoon—a madman that can't co-ordinate two ideas. Ah, blockhead. (*Shaking his fist.*) I don't know how I keep my head. My breast is burning. My throat is dry. (*Pulls the bell.*) Teresa! eh! Teresa!

DOL. (*calling*). Teresa! (*Turning to* JUAN.) What's the matter?

JUAN. Nothing—nothing.

TERESA *entering*.

TER. Señor?

JUAN. Bring me a glass of sherry. No, a glass of water—water only.

TER. Yes, señor. [*Exit.*

JUAN (*walking about*). From this day I have to mortify myself—on bread and water, like an anchorite—all for Lazarus. Come, is not this to be put to my credit?

DOL. Yes; but much prudence. Let nobody know anything.

JUAN. Nothing. Our journeys will be journeys of pleasure; artistic voyages, that Lazarus may see the world and gain instruction. If all these were false terrors!

DOL. Not a word to anybody.

JUAN. Not to Carmen—say nothing to Carmen.

DOL. Poor Carmen, my poor angel! But you are right. The first is Lazarus.

JUAN. The first—that's clear. But that girl does not come, and I am choking.

Enter TERESA *and* DON TIMOTEO.

TER. (*announcing, and with the glass of water*). Here is Don Timoteo.

JUAN. Let him come in.

TER. He is already in.

JUAN (*to* DOLORES). Silence, and let us affect indifference.

DOL. (*aside*). Indifference and gaiety. (*Wiping her eyes.* DON JUAN *drinks a glass of water.*)

JUAN (*to* DOLORES). Will you take some ? Drink, dear. Be calm ! [*Exit* TERESA.

DOL. Thank you ; I am calm now.

TIM. Doña Dolores !

DOL. Friend Don Timoteo !

JUAN. My dear Timoteo ! (*Wishing to embrace him.*)

TIM. Don't embrace me. Don't you see that I have come according to etiquette ? All in black !

DOL. In black ! Why?

JUAN. Why?

TIM. Don't be alarmed ; it is not mourning, but etiquette. I come in all solemnity. Now you shall see. Isn't Carmen here?

DOL. We went together to hear Mass. She came back with me—and she is now in my sitting-room with Don Nemesio and with Javier—so merry !

TIM. Then let everybody come here ! (DOLORES *rings the bell.*) Everybody — except Lazarus ; he must come afterwards. Ah ! solemnity ! solemnity ! (*Laughing.*)

TER. (*entering*). Señora . . .

DOL. Let the Señorita Carmen have the goodness to come here.

TIM. She and all—all. And till they come let no one speak to me.

DOL. (*aside to* DON JUAN). Don't you guess?

JUAN (*aside*). Yes. [*A pause.*

TIM. Solemn silence! Silence, a precursor of something very grave. Ha! ha!

Enter CARMEN, NEMESIO, *and* JAVIER.

CAR. (*to her father*). Did you call me?

TIM. Silence, little one. Don't you see how grave we all are?

CAR. But what's the matter?

TIM. (*to his daughter*). You stand beside Dolores.

A movement among all: CARMEN *embraces* DOLORES.

So: that's well.

DOL. My own daughter!

JUAN (*aside*). God assist me!

NEM. Ah—ha!

JAV. (*to* NEMESIO). We are having a wedding.

TIM. Silence!—Are we ready? All attention—and every solemnity—for I am going to begin. Ah! you, Javier, being the youngest man here, shall go out in haste at the fitting moment to find Lazarus—" Lazarus! Lazarus!" You understand?—So, so—all very quiet: hanging on my lips. (*A pause.*) Señor Don Juan Mejia—(*with comic solemnity*.) My dear sir—The devil, I seem as if I were going to write a letter! —Juanito, you asked me for the hand of Carmen for Lazarus: I have consulted the girl, she is dying about the boy, and now I bring the girl to the boy. And I say before all—Let them be married—the devil—let them be married!—(*with great energy*.)—The programme in these cases—gentlemen, the programme.

—The blushing, the weeping, the smiling, the embracing!

(*All spontaneously go through the instructions.* CARMEN *and* DOLORES *embrace, and* DOLORES *weeps passionately.* NEMESIO *and* JAVIER *laugh while pointing out the groups.* TIMOTEO *and* NEMESIO *likewise embrace. Then* TIMOTEO, *as if recollecting himself, continues—*)

Javier—go and look for Lazarus—Away, the situation is falling flat!

JAV. I am off—I am off! Lazarus! Lazarus!
[*Exit.*

CAR. Mother!

DOL. My own daughter — my own daughter! (*Aside.*) My God! My God!

TIM. (*to* DON JUAN). And you say nothing?

JUAN. Why, nothing more was required.

TIM. But he is not coming.

Re-enter JAVIER *and* LAZARUS; *the latter pale, disordered, and materially dragged along by the former.*

LAZ. Where are you taking me? Where?

JAV. Come, man, come . . . to happiness!

LAZ. What's this? What do they want with me? Why do they call me?

TIM. *Tableau!* Carmen is yours! I bring her to you! You are to be married! (*To* DON JUAN.) Eh! you father of a cork-tree, say something to them; I have gone through all my part!

LAZ. Carmen—she—is it true? My Carmen!

DOL. Your Carmen—she is yours.

JUAN. What the devil! She is yours—be happy, and let the world founder! what do I care for the world!

5

Laz. Mine, mine! I may go to her! fold her in my arms! embrace her with all my soul! drink her in with my eyes! I may if I like?

Juan. Yes! enough that you say—yes!

Laz. Oh, the infamy of it! Oh, the treachery! Carmen!

Car. (*going up to him*). Lazarus!

Laz. No, keep off! To whom are you coming? You are not to be mine! Never—never—never!

Car. He casts me off! He casts me off! I knew it! Mother! mother! (*Falls into the arms of* Dolores.)

Dol. Daughter of my heart!

Tim. My daughter! What have you done? What have you done?

Nem. But I don't understand.

Jav. I do.

All hasten to help Carmen.

Juan. Lazarus—my son!

Laz. (*embracing his father*). Father—father—you are my father, save me!

Juan. Yes, I shall save you—I gave you life!

Laz. You gave me life! But that's not enough: give me more life—to live, to love, to be happy—give me life for my own Carmen—give me more life, or cursed be the life which you gave me!

[*Falls insensible.*

END OF ACT II.

ACT III.

The scene represents a room in the country seat of DON JUAN, *on the banks of the Guadalquivir, in accordance with the description in the earlier part of the first act, although with some pieces of furniture of a more recent period and of more sober taste. There still remain some divans, the carpet and various objects of art. Furthermore, a little table and a low chair. In the background is a balcony or terrace, which is understood to encircle the building. There is an ample view of the sky and of the horizon. If the balcony can be made to slope somewhat towards the left, so much the better for the final scene. A door at the right, another to the left. A lounge to the right: to the left a sofa: a lighted lamp on some table to the side or at the back. It is night: the sky blue and starlight; as the act proceeds the lights of dawn gradually ascend.*

DON TIMOTEO, JAVIER and PACA are discovered; the last named walks about the back and on the terrace as if to arrange something: she is dressed in a black or very dark costume: mantle[1] of black crape and with fringes.

[1] The original "pañolon" is a sort of cloak or shawl or blanket-like covering worn by Andalusian women.

Tim. And so Dolores wrote to you?

Jav. Yes, señor. Lazarus wished to see me: my company was very much wanted to hasten on his convalescence: he was talking constantly about me. Finally, I said: "I must go there," I took the train, and two hours ago I planted myself at the door of this country seat, of this delightful country seat; which ought to have admirable views, as far as I have been able to judge by the feeble light of the stars.

Tim. But didn't you know it? Weren't you acquainted with Don Juan's country seat?

Jav. No, señor.

Tim. (*waggishly*). I was. I have known it for many years. I knew it—ay, when Juan and I were young men! When I used to call him Juanito, and he called me Timoteito. Ah, ah! (*mysteriously.*) What a number of reminiscences these venerable precincts awaken! All that you see is impregnated with love and madness, with alcohol and merriment. I could tell you: on this divan Juan one day fell down drunk: in that corner I fell one night in the same condition: and on that balcony we both fell one morning in a similar situation. Oh, most sacred memories! Oh, beloved images of the past! (*To* Paca). What are you doing here?

Paca. I am putting everything in order, señor.

Tim. And now you will see such a panorama. That balcony looks toward the East, and you see the Guadalquivir—" Sevilla, Guadalquivir, how you do torment my mind!" The loveliest girls of the Sevillian land have breakfasted here, have danced here, have sung here, and have got drunk here.

Jav. Ah, ha! you amused yourselves here in fine style.

Paca *sighs*.

TIM. (*turning round in ill humour*). Have you not done? Have you not done, Paca.

PACA. Well, I remained to see—if you gentlemen wanted anything, that's all.

TIM. Nothing, you may go to the kitchen.

PACA. Very well, Don Timoteo: to the kitchen. Ah! my God! (*She takes a low chair on to the terrace, sits down and fans herself.*)

TIM. I tell you that I can look at nothing which surrounds me without being moved. The girls from Sevilla, the girls from Malaga, the girls from Tarifa! But let us make a full stop. I am perverting you, young man: and at my age that's a villainous thing. But the fact is that there were certain girls from Sevilla and Malaga and Cadiz, and certain girls from Tarifa.

PACA *gives a very big sigh on the balcony.*

Who's that sighing? The devil of a woman, there's nothing dismal in what we are saying—are you here still?

PACA (*from the balcony and without rising*). To see if Don Timoteo wanted anything.

TIM. I do want something, and this gentleman wants something. Bring us a few glasses.[1]

PACA *rises and approaches.*

JAV. Many thanks: they gave me supper a short time ago: it is now very late—and I take nothing at such an hour as this. (*To* PACA.) Don't trouble yourself on my account.

PACA. Then.

[1] "Glasses." The word in the original, throughout this act is cañas or canitas. These are conical-shaped glasses from which Spaniards drink Manzanilla—a lighter wine than sherry.

TIM. Then, trouble yourself on my account Go go, and bring that.

PACA. Yes, señor, yes; I am going, Don Timoteo.

[*Exit fanning herself.*

JAV. Good heavens! Manzanilla at this hour?

TIM. Yes, yes, of course, I know that you are very steady. Lazarus writes dramas; you write history; but, my friend, a glass is taken at any historical moment whatever.

JAV. At any historical moment? But one o'clock in the morning, although it be an exquisite morning of summer, is that an historical moment or a moment to go to sleep?

TIM. For the pleasure of tasting, eh? for the pleasure of tasting a sweet little drop of Manzanilla, the twenty-four hours of this day, and the twenty-four of the following, and those of the next, are marked down in all treatises, young man. Admit that there are no young men nowadays.

JAV. How can it be helped? There are young men who are old, and there are old men who die quite young.

TIM. It's true. Since I came eight days ago to the country seat, my remembrances have become refreshed, and I feel as if I were fifteen years old.

JAV. And in a few more days you'll feel as if you were fifteen months.

TIM. Halloa! Halloa! that figure of speech is called irony.

JAV. A respectful irony, Don Timoteo. But I did not think to meet you at the country seat of Don Juan.

TIM. I had brought poor Carmen to Sevilla. She is very delicate. With those unfortunate events— with the illness of Lazarus—and what you know already. But when once at Sevilla, Juanito was anxious that we should come and pass a few days here. And I, to give that pleasure to Carmen, and to contribute to the recovery of Lazarus—who, they declared, was going on very well—I consented and here we are.

JAV. Restored to youth.

TIM. Believe me, Javier, in what I told you just now: there is no longer any youth now: Carmen with her afflicted little chest: Lazarus with his disordered nerves; you with your sedateness and your megrim. We were of another stamp.

JAV. Perhaps it's because you were of another stamp, that we are made after this fashion. But let us change the subject, Don Timoteo. And so there is a complete reconciliation, and a wedding in perspective?

TIM. I'll tell you, I'll tell you. But that Paca is not bringing the Manzanilla. (*Looking to see if she comes.*) Really there was no cause to be offended. Lazarus said what he said—in a fever! You saw him fall senseless at the feet of Carmen. What the devil was the meaning of that? Go and learn that. In my time when a man fell down thus, it was decided to be drunkenness or apoplexy, and so medical science became simplified and was within the reach of everybody. But in these days, interpret you who can what's the matter with the man who falls insensible.

JAV. Poor Lazarus was very ill. However, they say that he is now getting on perfectly: the malady has passed the critical point.

TIM. So they say and he seems very much restored: but he is always a very extraordinary person—like all men of talent.

JAV. And so we shall have the wedding.

Tim. Hum—wedding—that's flour from another sack. I say nothing so as not to distress Carmen, not to be disagreeable to the parents, and because I would not give the boy another fainting fit. If Lazarus recovers completely and comes back to what he was, and writes something that will bring him considerable fame—sufficient to prove that his brain is quite sound—then the way is clear—eh? Because Carmen, poor Carmen. But this Paca is not coming!

Jav. Carmen is very fond of him, is she not?

Tim. I don't know—I don't know that girl, God help me! I am taking her away soon: within four or five hours we shall set out to catch the train. And before going away I shall speak to Bermudez.

Jav. I only saw Lazarus for a moment, and he seemed to me——

Tim. How?

Jav. Much better. Youth works miracles. (*Aside.*) Poor Lazarus!

Tim. It's true, it's true. I myself had—I don't know what—and I was so to say—crazy for more than a year—much more; and it passed off.

Jav. Well nobody would think it—I mean nobody would think that you had ever had—anything—of that kind of infirmity—eh?

Tim. Well, I had it, I had it—they believed that it had left me an idiot——

Jav. Jesus, Mary, and Joseph!

Tim. But that devil of a woman who is not coming! She knew quite well that the Manzanilla was only for me, and she delights in mortifying me. She has a most perverse mind. And she was always the same; you don't know what that woman has been!

Jav. Who? She who was here just now?

Tim. Exactly; that was one of the most magnificent

women in all Andalusia. She was called Paca the Tarifeña.

JAV. Ah ha ! who would have said so !

TIM. I should have said so, Juanito would have said so, Nemesio would have said so, and everybody would have said so. The Tarifeña ! the girl from Tarifa !—she who acts in this house to-day as a servant or little better, twenty or thirty years ago commanded like a mistress. Afterwards, as always happens, she rambled about—rambled about—and farewell beauty, farewell grace, farewell magnificence. Old age, ugliness and misery, the three enemies—I'll not say of the soul, but of the bodies of pretty girls, fed themselves upon the gay Tarifeña. Five or six years ago Juan got to know of it ; he felt sorry, and he took her into this country house, as mistress of the keys or something—as a matter of form. In short, she is in service in the country seat ; but she will not be of much service, for she was always very lively, but very lazy.

JAV. Yet, so beautiful ?

TIM. A sun ! But women break down early. We men preserve ourselves better. Who would say that I am fifty-eight years old ?

JAV. Nobody ! Whatever else you may be accused of—(*Aside.*) Seventy-five !

TIM. I should think so. Halloa ! I think Lazarus is coming.

Enter LAZARUS *on the left. Behind comes* Doctor BERMUDEZ, *but at a certain distance from* LAZARUS, *as if observing him and being on the watch.*

LAZ. (*looking at* DON TIMOTEO *and* JAVIER). This night we are all sitting up, the sitting up of the farewell.

TIM. I am obliged to you, but there was no need for you to trouble yourself. Let us say farewell now: you go to bed: and Carmen and I at daybreak, very quietly, without rousing anybody, will set out for the train.

LAZ. So, so; very quietly, without waking anybody, in the silence of the night: so you wish to steal Carmen away. And so happiness is stolen away. Treachery! But I am watching and I shall watch: Lazarus has risen, and now he will never sleep any more. These eyes are very wide open to see everything (*tenderly*): the dear little head of my Carmen (*laughing*), the great, villainous head of Don Timoteo. To see the day with its splendour and the night with its gloom. (*Going to the balcony.*) How beautiful is the morning star—is it not? It is always there. We seem to have made an appointment with each other. "I shall appear in heaven," she says, "and do you appear at the balcony, and we shall gaze upon each other." I cannot gaze upon you, forgive me; Carmen would be jealous. She not being at my side, I do not wish to gaze on anybody, I do not care to see anybody. (*Withdraws irritably from the balcony and sees* BERMUDEZ.) Halloa, dearest doctor, were you here? Did you follow me? Did they send you to take charge of me? Well, look you, it annoys me to have a sentinel always in sight—(*Restraining himself and changing his tone*) unless he be so kind hearted as my dear doctor.

They all advance to the first entrance.

BERM. I came with you to beg you not to sit up. Now go to bed, take some rest, and at daybreak I shall awaken you that you may bid good-bye to Carmen and to Don Timoteo.

LAZ. That's what you want! I am not a child: I am not to be deceived. How does he who sleeps know what he will see on his awaking? If he does awake! (*Sits down.*)

TIM. However. (*Approaching him.*)

JAV. (*approaching still nearer*). I give you my word. . . .

BERM. (*All surround him.*) We all promise you solemnly——

LAZ. It is useless — don't trouble yourselves. Besides I neither believe anybody, nor trust in anybody. I don't trust myself, and I am always observing myself whether perchance—in short, I understand myself: then how should I trust you? You perceive that that's asking too much. And enough, enough— I have said no.

BERM. As you please, Lazarus.

LAZ. Moreover, sitting up is delightful. What a sky! what a night, what a river! Just now we were downstairs in the drawing-room that looks on to the garden, my mother, my father, Carmen, the doctor, I—(*counting on his fingers*) and Paca likewise. All seated, all resting, and somewhat sleepy, excepting Paca. In an angle a lamp: the doors on a level with the outside: the sky in the distance: the garden with its twining plants and its rose trees making itself a portion of the saloon, as if to bear us company: the penetrating perfumes of the lemon flower, and the freshness of the river impregnating the atmosphere: little insects of all colours, a few butterflies among them, as if engendered by the air, came from without, attracted by the lamp, and fluttered between the light and the gloom, as ideas revolve within me now; and Paca too was fluttering amidst us all. (*A pause.*) What, you are laughing? (*To* JAVIER.)

Jav. I am not laughing.

Laz. Yes; you laugh because I said that Paca was fluttering between my father, my mother, Carmen and myself. Well, I maintain it: is it only butterflies that flutter about? Flies and gad-flies flutter as well. And so, as I lay there with eyes half closed, Paca, with her black dress and her black mantle with its fringe, seemed to me an enormous fly. She fluttered ponderously from my father to my mother—serving my father with sherry and my mother with iced water —and between Carmen and myself, to worry me with questions, and to fix a flower in Carmen's hair, rustling against us both with her mantle and its fringes, as a fly rustles with its dark and hairy wings. She is a kind woman but I felt a repugnance, a loathing, and a chill, and I came up to stand and breathe on yonder balcony.

Jav. And to contemplate the stars.

Laz. One, no more than one. And such extravagant ideas! But we apprentices of poetry are thus. You are right, Bermudez, extravagant—very—very—. I was thinking of Paca, I was gazing at the star, and I felt an insane, ridiculous, but unconquerable desire. It was to seize one of my foils, to run it through the gad-fly with her fringed mantle, as one runs an insect through with a pin, and to burn her at the light of that most beautiful star. Like what? The putrescence of humanity which is consumed and purified in heavenly flames. You don't understand me, Don Timoteo?

Tim. Well, I don't think there is much to understand — and even though a man may not be a genius——

Laz. Don't be vexed: these are jokes: I offend you? The father of Carmen? when for her sake I am ready to go down on my knees and to declare that you are young and beautiful and that you have brains, and to compel the whole world to declare the same. Your arms, Don Timoteo, your arms. (*They embrace.*) You bear no grudge against me, do you?

TIM. Dear me, why should I?

LAZ. Then don't take away Carmen; don't separate me from her. A sick man should have his way in everything — and it would make me worse, let Bermudez tell you. Is it not true that it would make me ill? Say it—say it?

TIM. But you are well now?

BERM. Quite well.

LAZ. And you, what do you say?

JAV. My boy, I find you as well as ever.

TIM. And I really must go to Sevilla. But we shall soon come back to be reunited. You are not a convalescent: you don't require to stay here. Away home to work!

LAZ. (*in the ear of* TIM.). Then when shall the wedding be?

TIM. For my part—any day—but that, let the doctor say.

LAZ. Not that man—not that man—ah—I know him —and yet let him say.

BERM. It depends on the state of mind that you are in: if you are in a sound state of mind, very soon.

LAZ. Well, before you take Carmen away you have to decide it. The morning approaches—it will be here in less than two or three hours. You see that brightness? It is beginning to dawn already, and we must sit up by all means. Therefore you go in there, into that cabinet—and you fix the date. I shall not be in your way. Now you see that I can do no more. But you must say when and let me know; when I know it I shall be more at ease. With to-day there will be one day less: two less: three—it is not far off now: very little short of the time: three days off, two days off, one day off, it is to-morrow, it is to-day—she is my Carmen for ever—she is mine—(*vehemently*). Now, let who dare force her from my arms! Oh! Carmen now belongs to Lazarus. (*Changing his tone.*) I am saying what will happen—when you fix the day—because by the fixing of the day we only want two—now we are only short of one—now it has arrived—all happy! (*Embracing* TIM. *and* JAV.). It's true, it's true! And now, in there.

TIM. For my part, with much pleasure, and it seems to me a good idea. Will you have it so, Bermudez?

BERM. I am at your orders—and if Lazarus insists——

LAZ. No more—no more—enter—here—and in all freedom. Your little cabinet—the balcony open—the flowers of that terrace which are beginning to take colour—the Guadalquivir which commences to waken with its silver lights. Very good—very good—you are going to be perfectly comfortable—and all this will incline you to good nature. Don't be very cruel —don't fix too long a term—for in this world, what is not to-day is never.

TIM. Shall we go in?

BERM. Yes, señor.

They move slowly and speaking in low tones toward the right.

LAZ. (*in a low, energetic voice to* JAVIER). And you, too, go. I don't trust them. The wretches, they would say never: go, go, with them.

JAV. But I——

LAZ. (BERM. *and* TIM. *are now at the door*). Eh?

wait. Javier is accompanying you, I have requested him—because I wish to have some one who may plead for me and for Carmen. This you cannot deny me.

TIM. I should think not—come—come.

JAV. (*to* LAZ.). If you insist.

LAZ. In there, all three—all three—and afterwards we shall give an account of all to my mother and my father and Carmen. Quick—quick——

BERM. (*at the door*). You two go in——

TIM. You go in first.

BERM. By no means.

LAZ. Go in any way : I am waiting——

BERM. We shall soon have done. Be calm, Lazarus, be calm.

LAZ. (*alone*). Yes : he is right : I have need of much calm.—Outside there all is calm : then why should I not be calm as well? Without there is twilight (*pressing his forehead*) : within here is another twilight. But yonder half obscurity will end by filling itself with light. And this—this ? I seem to see beyond the luminous little clouds a great gloom. There without are worlds and suns and immensity—yet nothing of that bears the least consequence to me : here within are three insignificant persons—and it is they who are about to decide my destiny. To be menaced with the danger of one of those orbs that whirl through space overwhelming Carmen and myself—there would be grandeur for us in such a fate. But to be threatened with the possibility of a doctor and a fool putting me in a cage and leaving Carmen outside, to fret her pale front against the cold iron bars—this is cruel, this is humiliating—and nobody shall humiliate me. I am worth more than them all put together. I am better than them all. (*Interrupting himself.*) Better than Carmen ?—no. Neither am

I better than my mother. And my father—my father—he loves me much—more than I—silence! Yet if he is capable of loving more than I, then he is better than I—the result is that everybody is better than Lazarus. How is this possible? (*Walks about in great agitation.*)

Enter PACA *with some cups of Manzanilla.*

Who is this? It is Paca. Why the result will be—I see it—that even that creature is better than myself.

PACA. Is not Don Timoteo here? Then why does he give orders for nothing? He gives orders and then he goes away.

LAZ. Whom are you looking for?

PACA. For Don Timoteo: he asked me for some cups of Manzanilla, and he went away without waiting for me.

LAZ. Bring them, bring them. I'll take them. Leave them here.

PACA (*putting them on a little table*). You, señorito? And if they do you harm?

LAZ. Harm to me? Poor woman! Look—(*drinks a cup.*) I drink and you flutter about.

PACA. I flutter about, señorito? Ah! what things you say!

LAZ. What do you see out there?

PACA. Nothing.

LAZ. Just so. Nothing: that's what we all see. And inside here, what do you see?

PACA. Well, you.

LAZ. That's it, the son of Don Juan drinking; and Paca whirling around. (*Drinks another glass.*)

PACA. Don't drink any more, señorito: you are not at all well and it will do you harm. And Doña Dolores will be grieved and Don Juan will be grieved.

LAZ. And I'll make the Manzanilla grieve. And you, won't you be grieved?

PACA. Why yes: for I am very fond of the señorito.

LAZ. The result is that everybody is fond of me. Everybody is fond of me, and I am fond of nobody. Ah! of Carmen—yes: and of my mother as well: and of my father: and of poor Javier—well, then I am fond of everybody—This (*taking a cup or glass.*) must make it clear. (*Giving* PACA *a glass.*) Let us both make it clear.

PACA (*stopping him*). Señorito, for God's sake!

LAZ. No; it isn't for God's sake, it's for mine.

PACA. If you insist. (*Drinks.*)

LAZ. And now I. (*Takes up another glass.*)

PACA (*stopping him*). No; not you.

LAZ. Well then, you.

PACA. Ah! by the most Holy Virgin, you see I have lost the practice.

LAZ. You fool, why this is very healthy. It gives you strength. I now feel capable of anything. Awhile ago you seemed to me all funereal; now I perceive your black cloak to be all overspread with spangles of gold, and fragments of rainbow, like the wings of a butterfly.

PACA. Ah, señorito, I have been that. Ask——

LAZ. Ask whom?

PACA. Nobody—anybody whatever. Ugh, I am stifled. (*Lets fall the black handkerchief from her head over her shoulders.*) Yes, señorito—when people said—the Tarifeña—there was no need to say more.

LAZ. That was a climax, eh? Well, take another and you shall begin again.

PACA. You see we shall both be getting upset.

(*They take the glasses.*)

LAZ. Listen, Tarifeña, sylph of former times, enchanting siren of our forefathers, moth-eaten memorial of their joys, will you do me a favour?

PACA. I should think so. I am loyal to the house, and to all that's in the house, and to you, señorito, because you are of the house.

LAZ. Good; and to those who are not of the house, no. Well, inside there are three who are not of the house: Don Timoteo, Bermudez, and Javier. And those three are working so that I may not be married to Carmen. They say that I am ill, that I am a bad fellow, that I would cause much misery to Carmen; in short, they propose to break off my wedding—see what infamy!

PACA. Old men never wish young people to be married; old men are great scoundrels. Old women are quite the contrary; we old women would like everybody to get married. Why, what does the human race exist for? To get married; exactly. And you and beautiful little Carmen will make such a pair!

LAZ. You are very kind, very tender-hearted; you don't wish any one to suffer pain. Take this (*gives her another cup*)——

PACA. Ah! yes, señorito, although it doesn't become me to talk about my being tender-hearted, I never harmed any one.

LAZ. So ought all women with good hearts to be. Take——

PACA (*refusing it*). I can't take any more. I can't take any more.

LAZ. Then listen. That cabinet leads to the terrace, and the terrace goes round the house—you understand?—and the window which looks on to the terrace is on a level with it, so that if you go on to the terrace by here, and approach, you can hear everything; and if they wish to separate me from my own little Carmen, you come and tell me, and I'll know what to do.

PACA (*laughing*). What good ideas you have, señorito. I should think I would do this!—the vagabonds! But Don Juan wishes you to be married?

LAZ. Does he not wish it! The one who does not wish it is Don Timoteo. The one who wishes to carry off little Carmen as soon as daylight comes, is he! The one who means to strangle them all—is myself. And the one who has to make fools of them —that's you.

PACA. With the very greatest pleasure.

LAZ. But first of all go down to the garden, enter the drawing-room—my father and mother will be sleeping, Carmen will be awake; Carmen does not sleep, I know that!—and without any one but herself hearing you, tell her—that I am waiting for her; tell her to come up, that at dawn her father is taking her away, and that I want to bid her farewell. You understand?

PACA. Yes, señorito—— Farewell! Farewells are very sad. I have bidden farewell many times, and I have always wept.

LAZ. Good. Well now you shall weep again. We shall all weep.

PACA. Don't say that.

LAZ. Yes, you simpleton, weeping relieves you. Take note: laughing tires you, and weeping relieves you.

PACA. Well now it's true. Ah! what you do know, señorito!

LAZ. Take this (*giving her a glass*). You and I are also going to bid farewell to each other: clink—clink ex-Tarifeña.

PACA. To the health of the Señorita Carmen.

LAZ. To the health of the man whom you have most loved—when you were in love.

PACA. Then to the health—to the health of all the family!

LAZ. (*reversing the glass*). Look, not a drop!

PACA. The same with me.

LAZ. And now to call Carmen—and afterwards to listen to what those people say.

PACA. I am going there; give me another to take breath.

LAZ. Drink, my dear, drink.

PACA. You shall see what I am. (*Goes towards the cabinet.*)

LAZ. No, not that way; I told you by the terrace. (*Making her go out by the terrace.*)

PACA. Ha, ha! Yes, I shall know it all some day. He wants to show me the way of the house (*laughing*).

LAZ. Now quick; and first of all let Carmen come.

PACA. At once, at once; but don't make her cry, poor little thing, poor little thing; men like to make women cry; but she—she—is such a sweet little thing. Jesus, how warm it is! [*Goes out by the terrace.*

LAZ. (*alone*). I feel more confident—I find the strength flowing into my arms. To defend Carmen I need much strength. Well, I have it now. Everything is dawning—everything is rising—everything is returning. Light on the horizon, life to my muscles, and Carmen to me. Lazarus is Lazarus. The moment has arrived for the struggle—for the supreme struggle. But here one cannot struggle. Everything is soft and yielding. The carpet soft, the divans soft, the East filled with gauze and tufts of cotton wool. I want rock whereon to lean back, a sword to cut, a mace to crush—hardness, angles, metals that may offer resistance to me—and let me reduce all to powder (*pressing his forehead*). I feel the blood whirling round within my temples! (*pressing his bosom*) fire in my breast! engines of steel in my arms!

(CARMEN *appears on the terrace with* PACA *who points her out to* LAZARUS, *then disappears.*)

Carmen!

CAR. Lazarus!

LAZ. (*strains her frantically in his arms*). Carmen, my own Carmen. Now let them say what they like, those imbeciles, and let them come to seek you.

CAR. But what's the matter with you? My God! I don't understand.

LAZ. You don't understand that I love you more than my life, and that I have never told you so?

CAR. Yes, you have many times told me so.

LAZ. But in very poor fashion—coldly, lifelessly. The fact is that there is no way of saying these things. Commonplace words, commonplace phrases! "I love you more than my life, more than my soul; you are my happiness, you are my hope, my dream. . . ." Pshaw! Everybody says that. It has become profaned on all lips.

CAR. When I heard you speak so, it seemed to me that you were the only one in the world who said such things.

LAZ. No, you little goose, they all say them. And I don't wish to say what everybody says; because you are not like other people, and for you it is necessary to invent other things. Let me see, what shall I invent?

CAR. What you like. But while you are inventing, you may go on saying what you used to say, for it sounds well to me—and if it doesn't trouble you. . . .

LAZ. You will never have understood how I love

you, for I have not known how to explain myself; I have not understood it myself until now. I saw surrounding me an immeasurable horizon, and I was lost in the contemplation of it: worlds and marvels and splendours and sounds and melodies. But now all is obscured, all has become confined: a sombre background which folds itself up, something like a stupendous eyeball which becomes contracted, and in the centre nothing is left but a small circle of light, and in that circle is an image—it is yours;—now all has become blotted out, and there remains no more than Carmen, and in Carmen I reconcentrate all that lies before me of life, of longing, of thought, of love. Let not the eyeball close up finally, for then I shall be left in darkness.

CAR. Then you love me more than I thought? What joy for me!

LAZ. There is no reason to be joyful, for they wish to separate us.

CAR. Who?

LAZ. They. (*Pointing to the cabinet.*)

CAR. Why?

LAZ. Because I have not known how to explain to them what you are to me, and neither have you understood; and they believe that we shall console ourselves, that we shall grow resigned, that there is nothing more to be said than, "Lock up Lazarus, take away Carmen." Do you consent?

CAR. I? No, never; no, Lazarus, I am not resigned. I cannot do more than one thing: die. Well, I shall die. Can I do more?

LAZ. No; that will do well; that's enough.

CAR. But you can defend me.

LAZ. Defend you? How? Yes, I'll defend you; but how?

CAR. Why, who threatens us?

LAZ. I don't know. I can't well explain. I am now as it were on the boundaries of a desert; a desert contains much sand, which never ends; much solitude which is never filled; much thirst which is never quenched, and a sky which becomes flattened in the centre as if it were about to fall, and which never falls. At least if it did sink down all would be at an end.

CAR. Yes, much sadness which never ends. I felt that when I had doubts of you. It is true, the world was a desert.

LAZ. Well in that desert you gather up a handful of sand and you begin to count the little grains—one, two, three, hundreds, thousands—and you never finish counting. Yet there is no more than a handful—and you gather up another—and you gather up another—and the sand never ends. And you run and run; but no,—onward to the horizon all is overwhelmed with sand.

CAR. But what's the meaning of this? I don't understand.

LAZ. It means—it is very clear—don't you see? It seems clear to me, yet you don't understand. It means that I, who had wild dreams of applause, of glory, of gaining still more glory and applause with my Carmen, I see before me the fate of having to count grains and grains, handfuls and handfuls of sand, for days and nights and years, until the end—if there be an end. I don't know if there be an end.

CAR. Lazarus, Lazarus, don't talk so; don't look in that way!

LAZ. Then save me! Why what did I call you for except that you should save me?

CAR. Yes, I will save you; but how?

Laz. Consider now whether you love me so much. Suppose that we are about to say farewell for ever—because we are on the confines of that desert—both together at a little fountain—the last! It holds fresh water, the last! On the falling of the tube into the water it forms flakes of foam—the last—and I wish to drink for the last time and to cool my face and to sprinkle foam upon my lips that they may become wreathed in smiles. Help me—look at me—speak—laugh—sing—weep—do something, Carmen, for I am now being hurried away from you. I am now going into the desert; do something; throw me at least what your hands will hold of water, that a few drops may fall upon my face.

CARMEN *folds him in her arms.*

Car. But why do you say that? I don't understand. Are you sad? Are you vexed? Are you ill? These few days past, this very morning, you were so well, so cheerful, Lazarus.

Laz. They say—that I am going to forget you—that soon I shall not know you—that you will be close to me, and I—without suspecting it—like a child—like an idiot——

Car. No, not that!

Laz. But if it should be so?

Car. It will not be so.

Laz. Why not? (*His look begins to wander and he scarcely hears what follows; he assumes the face of an idiot and his arms fall to his sides.*)

Car. Because I shall be close to you—and will you not see me? Because I shall call to you "Lazarus!"—and will you not answer me? Because I shall weep much, my tears will fall upon you—and will you not feel them? I am weak as a child, but children too can hold on strongly. Lazarus, attend to me; are you not attending to what I say? I am Carmen. Look at me! That pale little head which you used to speak of is touching your lips. Look, I am smiling at you. Laugh yourself. Answer me. Lazarus—Lazarus—Awake! Do you hear me? What are you looking at?

LAZ. Yes—I know—I know—but call my mother.

CAR. No—I alone—they would separate us: we two alone. Why do you want your mother to come?

LAZ. I want to sleep.

CAR. (*looking on all sides*). Then rest on me. Sleep in my arms.

LAZ. You little fool, no. If I sleep it must be in the arms of my mother. That's what mothers are for. When I awake I shall call you.

CAR. Lazarus!

LAZ. Call her! Don't I tell you to call her? Obey, you selfish girl. Don't you wish that I should have rest neither?

CAR. Yes. I'll call her. (*Walking to the door.*) My God!

LAZ. Are you going or not? Or must I go myself?

CAR. No; wait; it is that I am not able. (*Standing at the door.*) Dolores! Don Juan!

LAZ. I said my mother—I only want one person; one.

CAR. Well, I was that one.

LAZ. No, she—I can't say to you—Mother!

CAR. (*calling*). Dolores!

LAZ. (*going towards her and calling*). Mother!

CAR. They are coming now.

LAZ. Several are coming. I did not say so many. I shall have to defend myself, and, to defend myself I need to have much courage. (*Drinks a glass.*)

CAR. Quick! Here! Dolores!

Enter DOLORES *and* DON JUAN.

DOL. Why did you call? Is it that Lazarus——?

JUAN. What's the matter with Lazarus?

LAZ. Nothing; Carmen was frightened—I don't know why, and she called.

CAR. He seems better. Lazarus, they are here now. Do you wish me to remain also?

LAZ. Why not? Yes, everybody about me. As we were downstairs. My mother, my father, sweet little Carmen, I! There's one short—ah! Paca. I still keep my memory. (*Laughing*.) Well, yes, we are short of Paca. Ha! Let us sit down as we were before, and let us wait till the day arrives. It is now about to dawn. Look, look what brightness there is in the distance. A great sitting up! And why are we sitting up?

DOL. You wished it——

JUAN. Yes, my son; it was you that insisted upon it; and when you desire anything, what are we all for but to give you pleasure?

LAZ. We have to bid farewell to Carmen. A farewell is a very sad and solemn thing, a thing beyond all consolation, and I have need to be consoled. Come, mother, to this side; come you also (*to his father*) to the other side; I must be between the two; and you must both tell me that this separation is a passing one, that we shall soon be all reunited to Carmen for ever—and, such other things as are said; though they may not be true they are said.

DOLORES *and* JUAN *are seated at either side of* LAZARUS.

DOL. But they are true.

JUAN. Why, nothing else was to happen.

CARMEN *approaches.*

CAR. Yes, Lazarus, we shall be reunited very soon.

LAZ. (*angrily*). You must not come near. You keep off.

CAR. (*withdrawing in pain and anguish*). Lazarus!

DOL. Lazarus, look how poor Carmen is grieved.

JUAN. Nay, come, my daughter, come; Lazarus wishes you to come.

LAZ. It cannot be. It is she who is going away. If she is going away she must be at a distance. And from a distance I say "Adieu, Carmen, adieu; I love you deeply." (*With passion.*) Do you see? It is not that I do not love her; it is that things must be as they are.

CAR. (*restraining her grief, aside*). Impossible! Impossible! My Lazarus!

DOL. (*to her son*). What's the matter with you?

JUAN. How are you, Lazarus?

LAZ. Very well; between you two, very well, as when I was a child, with the same calmness, the same peace as then.

DOL. You remember?

LAZ. Yes, for my head is very sound. With what clearness I remember those times!

JUAN (*to* DOLORES). You see? he is well, the same as during all those days. Carmen has alarmed herself without cause.

CAR. That's true, without cause.

JUAN. His head is far more steady than ours. This way—between the two.

LAZ. No. I remember everything now; between the two, no; I was alone with my mother; you were not there! Go away, go away. (*Putting his father away without violence.*)

JUAN. You don't remember that well, Lazarus. (*With humility.*) We were both beside you many times. (*In a tone of anguish.*) Is it not true, Dolores? (*In a supplicating manner.*)

DOL. Yes, my dear.

LAZ. No—I must not be contradicted. I was alone with her. (*Embracing her.*)

DOL. My son.

JUAN. Why do you put me away? Can I love you more than I do?

LAZ. Ah! yes—well, you are right, father.

JUAN. You see? I was right!

LAZ. Yes, once we were as we are now—ha, ha, ha!

JUAN. The same as now.

CAR. Oh, his look—his look! (*Aside.*)

LAZ. Hush—hush. As now—no, not as now. My mother was dishevelled, weeping, but very beautiful, and you haughty and disdainful, but gay and elegant. Away! and she weeping, sobbing, and you laughing; and you quarrelled—how you quarrelled! —it was terrible.

JUAN. No.

LAZ. Yes. I see it now.

CAR. (*aside*). His look! How he stares on every side!

JUAN. Don't be angry—but you don't remember well.

LAZ. (*angrily*). I must not be contradicted. You quarrelled. I know it—I see it—as I still feel that terror.

JUAN. Lazarus!

DOL. (*to* JUAN). Be quiet.

JUAN. Well, then we quarrelled—a little dispute.

LAZ. (*laughing*). No—no—it was not a little dispute. It was a desperate fight; you quarrelled in deadly earnest. And you, father, wished to take hold of me—and you took hold of me—and gave me a caress. (*Laughing.*) Come, come, you were not so bad.

JUAN. You see, Lazarus, you see?

LAZ. But my mother tore me out of your arms, and she pressed me in her own, and said to you: "Off with your hold; go away; go and enjoy yourself; go and get drunk. Leave him to me."

JUAN. No, Lazarus—I think not—as you were such a child you don't remember.

DOL. (*to* JUAN). Silence!

LAZ. And you cried out: "Well, then, remain with him, and much good may he do you! Much good!" What contempt! and you pushed me away.

JUAN. No, no, that I did not. I never did so.

LAZ. Yes.

JUAN. No.

LAZ. (*angrily*). I say yes. You pushed me—leave me, father; leave me alone with my mother. (*Putting him away.*) There, there, far off—far off—with Carmen.

JUAN (*withdraws and embraces* CARMEN). Oh, my Lazarus, my Lazarus!

LAZ. (*laughing, to his mother*). There are the exiles in their valley of tears.

CAR. It is not possible—it is not possible! Let them come—let them come; let them save him!

JUAN. Yes—let them save him.

LAZ. (*to his mother*). Now, with you.

DOL. With me—always with me.

LAZ. Always with you! No, that's not true neither. Why, Lord, you people don't remember anything; here nobody remembers a thing but myself. You sent me away—very far—to an accursed college. I wished to stay with you, and you said, "Let them take him away, let them take him away!" He (*pointing to his father*) said, "Stay with your mother," and he went away. You said, "Let them take him away," and you remained alone. Both, both of you separated yourselves from me. Oh, I remember all this very well, and until now I had never called it to mind. Something seems to be melting within my brain; something goes on sweeping away the ruins of all ideas of the present; and, as amid soil which the torrent drags along, there spring to light ancient moulds, so within here there rushes up the entire world of my childhood. So it is, and I remember everything. I fell asleep night after night without a kiss from either of you. Morning after morning I awoke without a caress from any one. Alone I lived—alone I shall continue to live; go, mother, to those yonder. (*Putting her away gently.*)

DOL. (*to* JUAN). Ah! through you! (*Turning back.*) Lazarus!

LAZ. I have said that I wish to be alone. I love you dearly, but take notice that things have to be precisely as they are.

DOL., CAR., *and* DON JUAN *are together;* LAZ. *contemplates them with a vague smile; then he continues.*)

Thus we are as we should be. Each one in his place —to every one his own. But I don't want to be so lonely either. Let Paca come—Paca!

JUAN. Whom is he calling?

LAZ. Her. Paca!

Enter PACA.

PACA. Señorito.

LAZ. Come; here—very close. (*To the others.*) Now I am not alone, you see, father? Now I have company, and merrier company than yours—you who are sad and gloomy as death. Take a glass, Paca, and give me another, and let us drink as we did a short time ago.

DOL. Lazarus!

PACA. Señorito, I drank a great deal, and now I don't know—now, my head is——

LAZ. Yes, I insist on it—you and I.

JUAN. Good God! No.

LAZ. Why not? Ah, you egoist, that have your own enjoyment and don't wish others to enjoy themselves. Well, I too wish to enjoy myself. My life is drawing to a close, and I must take advantage of that! Drink, Tarifeña, drink, and laugh, and dance, and twirl about. And tell me of your merry, youthful days—something that will cheer me, something to fire my blood, which I now feel turning cold. Laughter, orgies, dances, loves—something that may shake my nerves, which I now feel to be growing torpid. Come, Tarifeña, give me life, for I am young, and I wish to live.

JUAN. No more, no more—I cannot see this. I cannot bear this.

DOL. Oh, God!

JUAN (*rushes away from the others and approaches* PACA, *seizing her by an arm*). Go!

LAZ. (*holding her also*). She shall not go.

JUAN. I command it.

LAZ. And I also.

JUAN (*to* PACA). By the salvation of my soul, if you don't go, I shall throw you from that balcony into the river. Look, you don't know yet what I am. Quick!

LAZ. (*fiercely*). I have said no! Do you take a *e* light in tormenting me?

JUAN (*falling on his knees at the feet of his son*). Lazarus, for the love of God let this woman go away.

LAZ. Poor man! Ah! those white hairs. (*Fondling them.*) And he is weeping. Poor dear father! Well! you now see how grieved he is. Go away, woman, go away—since it must be so.

PACA withdraws.

JUAN. Oh—my Lazarus—my happiness—my chastisement!

LAZ. I don't want to chastise you; I don't want to chastise anybody. What I desire is that we should all be merry. Come, woman, you now see that nobody wants you; go away. Have you not heard?

PACA. First of all, I have to tell what those people (*pointing to the cabinet*) are saying; you ordered me.

LAZ. (*in astonishment*). I?

JUAN (*rises*). What do they say?

They all surround PACA.

PACA. Wicked things. That they won't let these two be married.

CAR. My God!

JUAN. Why? Speak!

DOL. Quiet!

JUAN. Say it low!

PACA. Because the señorito is about to have his last attack, and all will be at an end with him; and you —(*to* CARMEN) your father is now going to take you away.

DOL. Ah! (*runs to embrace her son, who has followed with his gaze the group.*)

CAR. (*desperately*). No! I—with him—for ever.

JUAN (*rushing to the cabinet*). Bermudez! Here!

PACA (*aside*). It's well that they should know it.

Enter BERMUDEZ, DON TIMOTEO *and* JAVIER.

JUAN. Bermudez—save my son and demand of me my life, my soul—all that you wish—what shall I not give you?—but save my Lazarus.

DOLORES *runs to meet* BERMUDEZ; CARMEN *alone remains with* LAZARUS.

DOL. Bermudez, one hope! One hope!

BERMUDEZ, *followed by* DOLORES *and* DON JUAN, *approaches* LAZARUS. TIMOTEO *advances towards* CARMEN. JAVIER *stands apart.*

TIM. Come, Carmen; my daughter, come. It is getting late.

CAR. No. With him; I'll not leave him so.

TIM. It is necessary—for heaven's sake, girl. (*Separating her from* LAZARUS.)

CAR. Lazarus, they are separating us.

LAZ. (*gathering himself together with a supreme effort.*) Who? That old man! That scum of the earth! Away, scum, to your heap of refuse! I pass on to life! I pass on to love! Carmen, to my arms! (*Rushes towards her, catches her, and takes her to the balcony. The others follow them.*) Look, what an horizon! What splendour! Come, melt your soul in mine, enfold your body round mine, and let us mingle ourselves among yonder rays of light. Yes, come, Carmen, come!

They are separated by force, and LAZARUS *is drawn away, and falls at last on the sofa.*

BERM. The last ray of light!

The characters are disposed of in the following manner:—LAZARUS *on the sofa to the right.* DON JUAN, *staggering, falls on the sofa to the left, hiding his face in his hands; as if to help him*, PACA *stations herself at his side. Toward the left* TIMOTEO *and* CARMEN; JAVIER *with* DOLORES *in the centre.* BERMUDEZ *stands contemplating* LAZARUS. *A pause.* LAZARUS *is motionless.*

JAV. (*in a low voice to* BERMUDEZ). Is he dead?
BERM. Would to God he were!
JUAN. How many mornings have I myself awakened here!
PACA. True!
JUAN. Silence!—And my Lazarus is not awaking.
DOL. (*to* BERMUDEZ). I have nothing left in life but Lazarus. In God's name, Bermudez, think of that.
TIM. Carmen!
CAR. It is useless, father. I shall not leave him.
BERM. Silence—silence! The day breaks—the sun begins to rise—Lazarus seems to be returning to himself. He lifts his gaze—he fixes it on the light which springs forth. Let us listen—let us listen!—This is decisive!
JUAN. To hear what he will say? Will he call upon me?
DOL. It is on me that he will call.
CAR. He will not call on me!
LAZ. (*with his face towards the rising sun*). Mother!
DOL. (*running to him and embracing him*). Lazarus!
LAZ. (*pointing to the sun*). How beautiful!
JUAN (*falling on his knees by the sofa and raising his arms:* PACA *holds him*). Lord! Lord!
DOL. Lazarus!
LAZ. Most beautiful! most beautiful! Mother—give me the sun!
DOL. Ah!—My God!
LAZ. The sun!—the sun!—I want the sun!

JUAN (*still on his knees; falls against the sofa:* PACA *holds him*). My boy!

DOL. (*embracing* LAZARUS). My darling!

CAR. (*wildly embracing her father, who subdues her*). Lazarus!—My life!

BERM. For ever!

LAZ. Mother—the sun!—the sun!—give me the sun! (*He says this like a child, and with the face of an idiot.*)

JUAN. I also asked for it. Jesus!—my Lazarus, my Lazarus!

LAZ. Give me the sun! Mother, mother—the sun! For God's sake—for God's sake—for God's sake, mother—give me the sun!

THE END.

www.ingramcontent.com/pod-product-compliance
Lightning Source LLC
Chambersburg PA
CBHW020110170426
43199CB00009B/470